Peer Coaching for Educators

Second Edition

Barbara Gottesman

The Scarecrow Press, Inc.
Technomic Books
Lanham, Maryland, and London
2000

SCARECROW PRESS, INC.
Technomic Books

Published in the United States of America
by Scarecrow Press, Inc.
4720 Boston Way
Lanham, Maryland 20706
http://www.scarecrowpress.com

4 Pleydell Gardens, Folkestone
Kent CT20 2DN, England

Copyright © 2000 by Barbara Gottesman

British Library Cataloguing in Publication Information Available

Library of Congress Cataloging-in-Publication Data
Gottesman, Barbara Little.
  Peer coaching for educators / Barbara Gottesman.—2nd ed.
    p. cm.
  Includes bibliographical references.
  ISBN 0-8108-3745-5 (paper : alk. paper)
    1. Teaching teams—United States. 2. Mentoring in education—United States. I. Title.

LB1029.T4 G68 2000
371.14'8—dc21

00-022128

⊗™ The paper used in this publication meets the minimum requirements of
American National Standard for Information Sciences—Permanence
of Paper for Printed Library Materials, ANSI/NISO Z39.48–1992.
Manufactured in the United States of America.

For Kevin
and
all the other Peer Coaches

CONTENTS

FOREWORD

While I was governor of South Carolina, we passed the Education Improvement Act (EIA) of 1984. The EIA reforms included research by Ron Edmonds on effective schools and positive school climate. The Effective Schools Training program resulted from Edmonds's indicators of school effectiveness and involved 377 schools in South Carolina. Peer Coaching is one of the staff development programs that has evolved out of the Effective Schools Training and has as its purpose to advance the professionalism of teachers by training them to observe, give feedback, and coach each other. Peer Coaching promotes the culture of collegiality among teachers in schools and in their professional development, which will do much to improve the quality of our schools and contribute to the success of the "Goals 2000: Educate America Act," our national reform plan.

Richard W. Riley
*The Secretary of the United States
Department of Education*

ACKNOWLEDGMENTS

The present author wishes to thank all of the people who have assisted in the development of this second edition of *Peer Coaching for Educators,* chiefly Dr. James O. Jennings. Buddy Jennings worked as my partner in the Effective Schools Training program as we fine-tuned the specific application of Peer Coaching when we both worked at the South Carolina Department of Education. Dr. Jennings also co-authored the first edition of *Peer Coaching for Educators.*

In addition to Governor Richard Riley who set in motion the Education Improvement Act of 1984 which made such programs as the Effective Schools Training possible, Dr. James O. Ray deserves many thanks for his leadership in principal and teacher staff development. Dr. Phyllis Crain also deserves thanks for peer coaching the creative process by reflecting on the many trials and errors that occurred as we worked to refine this concept. To these and to all the educators who took the risk to peer coach and let us know what worked and did not work in their school or college, we owe many thanks.

INTRODUCTION by Roland S. Barth

I had the good fortune to be "peer coached" by Barbara Gottesman and one of her colleagues—a memorable day. The experience reminded me then, as the book you are reading does now, of just how limited and primitive are learning experiences for adults in school—and how much richer the learning of educators can and must become. You can't lead where you won't go. Teachers, principals, and professors cannot lead our students toward profound learning until we ourselves go there. Peer coaching offers a remarkable vehicle for us to join with students as learners and together build a community of learners.

There exists within our school cultures a debilitating taboo against practitioners making their work mutually visible. All too often, we don't talk about our practice with others who engage in the same work; we don't observe others who do what we do; we don't ask for help, even when we desperately need it; and we rarely take responsibility for and invest ourselves in the success of our peers. Rather, we occupy what one teacher called "our separate caves." And for many good reasons. The world of schools makes us competitors for scarce resources and recognition. If I help you, you will do better and get more and I might do worse and get less.

And, as I recall from my days of teaching fourth and fifth grades, we all know we are living to some extent a lie. We know we are not doing all of what we are supposed to do and doing it well. We can't. So to invite scrutiny of our work is to invite discovery. To reveal oneself is to reveal one's flaws. In such an isolated, fearful, and vulnerable world, how can the performance of adults improve so that the performance of youngsters will improve?

Enter Peer Coaching—a powerful process whereby professional educators can assist and be assisted by fellow educators of equal status. Unlike other, perhaps safer and less influential forms of professional development, such as workshops, course work, and readings, which usually sit the learner on the bench observing the learned playing on the field, Peer Coaching demands that the teacher and administrator alike get onto the field where they get a chance to play—and to be coached. One assumes major risks when one gets off the bench and into the game. And one experiences extraordinary excitement, satisfaction, and learning.

With the careful framework provided here, it becomes clear that most risks are perceived risks, which soon turn into opportunities. Peer Coaching is nonevaluative, voluntary, and controlled largely by the learner. The person who is coached determines whether, when, and for how long, and for what purpose, the coaching will occur. Control and ownership, so foreign to conventional supervision, unlock abundant professionalism, support, and learning for the coach and the coached alike.

It's all here: a thoughtful rationale for Peer Coaching; what it is and what it isn't; who does what and in what sequence; how to get it all going within the schoolhouse; and why a system *should* get it going. And you will find, as I have, the concept of Peer Coaching presented with clarity, economy, honesty, and conviction. We should expect nothing less from an author who has lived and continues to live Peer Coaching. From "Where do I sit when I come into your classroom?" to the use of body language, to the building of trust between two individuals, the specifics are here. From the many sample simulations, the reader can experience exactly what might be said in the coaching dialogue.

Peer Coaching provides us, then, with an opportunity to promote frequent, informal, helpful observations by one professional educator to another. And it provides something even more valuable. By embedding adult, mutual visibility and learning into the fabric of the schoolhouse, Peer Coaching can transform the very nature of the school culture from a place where some are transmitting learning to others to a place where everyone engages in the most important enterprise of the schoolhouse—learning. That, it seems to me, is what good education is all about.

I suspect this tidy, approachable little book will be of great value not only to classroom teachers and school administrators but also to central office personnel and university faculty committed to promoting adult development within the schools. I hope so. Through Peer Coaching, we *can* lead where we *will* go.

CHAPTER 1 ×ᵖ

Experiencing Peer Coaching

WHY PEER COACHING?

Attacks on schools and teachers are as commonplace these days as mudslinging in political campaigns. Education is frequently the top priority for successful candidates because it is an easy issue for the public to understand. Everyone is an expert on education because she or he has experienced twelve or so years of schooling.

The simple political promises of a gubernatorial or presidential candidate become complex problems when he or she gains office and reforms are imposed. Reform in education has failed with predictable regularity. The bright promise of charter schools has dimmed, with many facing financial ruin or low enrollment. Vouchers will have their day also.

The people who often consider educators arrogant for thinking they know something about education never consider pediatricians arrogant for being experts on children's health. The purpose of this revised edition of *Peer Coaching for Educators* is to advocate a teacher-controlled method for improving instruction that works from within the school and has years of teacher experience to document its success.

In any given school, the accumulated years of training and experience of professional educators amounts to between six hundred and two thousand years. Granted, not all of it is masterly teaching experience or training, but the greatest resource in a school is still the brainpower and problem-solving ability of the human beings who comprise the school community. In the sixties, television in every classroom was the panacea. In the nineties, computers for every student and teacher will solve all the problems. Not! For future citizens to function successfully in an American democracy, their education must be interactive with adult problem-solving teachers. The computer, like television, must be a tool to master and command, not a replacement for interaction with teachers.

1

The Peer Coaching I have used and advocate for the improvement of instruction is an interactive, simple, nonthreatening structure that teachers use to help each other within the school. Teachers are not the only ones, however, who use Peer Coaching to improve the learning situation. My colleague James O. Jennings, Ph.D., and I have peer coached each other as staff development trainers, coached principals and other trainers conducting faculty meetings or presenting other staff development models, and served in the Goodlad National Network for Educational Reform as college deans.

The Peer Coaching model we designed owes a great deal to clinical supervision as practiced by Cogan, Goldhammer, and Hunter, but we have taken the away the aspects of supervision to make it peer-to-peer feedback and coaching for the improvement of instruction. This Peer Coaching model has five simple steps, which are illustrated with actual coaching sessions.

In our experience, it takes about four sessions to learn to effectively use the steps and the safety net of the rules for "No Praise, No Blame." In four more sessions, the coach and teacher feel comfortable with the process. After that, each pair begin almost daily, subconscious use of the Peer Coaching process. Instruction in the school begins to improve.

Evaluation and staff development do have their place in helping teachers to master new teaching skills or to grow and develop as beginning teachers. I advocate changing the culture of a school by Peer Coaching. Teachers can first pair up within grade levels or departments, but soon Peer Coaching can cross subject matter and grade levels. One of the most successful Peer Coaching sessions I had as an English teacher was in Colleton County (South Carolina), coaching a welding teacher in the vocational center!

In my experience, evaluation systems are useful for issues of contracts and termination, but Peer Coaching is more useful than evaluation for improvement of instruction. Staff development programs are great: teachers need to learn new skills. Most staff development models, however, consist of experts blowing in, blowing off, and blowing out, leaving teachers to follow up and problem solve among themselves. Therefore, many new models do not "take" in a school because there is no expert problem-solver present every day.

Peer Coaching can improve the success rate of new staff development models by having teachers coach each other in the new methods. Peer Coaching is a structure that can be used with any content material, for mastery of new methods, or for specific behavioral problems. Since the teacher "requests the visit" or observation, he or she can pinpoint the problem on which he or she wishes feedback and coaching. This method is easier that a supervisor's evaluation or clinical supervision process because it allows the teacher to work on a specific skill, the mastery of which is a work in progress, with no fear of evaluation.

Dr. Jennings, superintendent of the Spartanburg (S.C.) 2 School District, sees it this way:

> Recent research has stressed the importance of the teacher's role as it relates to the success of students. More than any variable besides the home, the quality of the teacher was found to be the single most important factor in determining how well students perform on standardized tests. The research suggests that the influence of the teacher goes beyond the one year the teacher has the student. Contact with a low-quality teacher may take several years to overcome, if it is overcome at all. To further complicate the problem is the fact that the low-performing students usually get the low-performing teachers.
>
> If this research is accurate, and we have no reason to believe that it is not, how do we ensure that all our students receive top-quality teachers? The first idea that would come to most people's minds is that of evaluation. We believe that our evaluation systems have been designed to observe teachers and then to fix or weed out those who do not belong in teaching. While, in theory, this may sound fine, in reality, it does not work. The failure of our current evaluation systems are well documented. Most school districts will tell you that few teachers are fixed or weeded out using the current evaluation systems.
>
> Teaching is a very complex and complicated skill. During any given day, most teachers will make hundreds of highly subjective decisions involving teaching and learning. To further complicate this matter is the fact that most teachers work in isolation. Therefore many critical decisions about teaching and learning are made in total and complete isolation.
>
> While it is not uncommon for other professionals to work in isolation, their isolation usually differs from that of teachers. In other professions, such as law and medicine, the professionals have an opportunity to work in teams to solve difficult cases. In the teaching profession, this practice is almost nonexistent and usually occurs in a non-structured, informal setting, if it occurs at all. Therefore we fail in education to develop an environment that promotes teacher growth. We have failed to provide the type of environment where teachers are encouraged to discuss teaching and learning in order to develop ideas and practice. If teachers were flowers, they would die on the vine for lack of nourishment. It should come as no surprise that many teachers make most decisions based on instinct rather than research. Most are about as skilled as they will ever be by the fifth year of teaching.

We must provide structures that will reduce the amount of time teachers spend in isolation. These structures must provide teachers the opportunity to interact with other teachers to identify, discuss, and implement ways to improve student success. Much of this must be done in a nonthreatening environment where people can share their successes, failures, and fears.

Despite what we know, most people still believe that supervisor feedback is the most effective, and many times the only, way to promote teacher growth. While this model does have some advantages and may motivate some people, it also has a tendency to have a negative effective on many others. Nonevaluative feedback, like Peer Coaching, is more likely to result in teacher reflection, teacher growth, and teacher change.

Accountability systems should be built on the premise that teacher growth will take place as a result of going through this process. While teachers may experience some limited growth as a result of the supervision model, little prolonged effect will take place and usually is set aside until the next time evaluation takes place. Only a model that reduces isolation and promotes self-evaluation and reflection can hope to promote substantial teacher growth.

A model such as Peer Coaching treats teachers like professionals and recognizes their needs. This model promises teachers the opportunity to explore other teaching techniques and learning opportunities in a safe environment. An environment that encourages sharing is a dialogue rich in context in order to improve teacher performance. *(October 1998)*

I am not advocating the elimination of the supervision-feedback model. Certainly there are times when this model is appropriate and even necessary, such as when termination issues arise. What I am advocating is a model that incorporates Peer Coaching as well as a supervisory model. This would allow schools to deal with teachers in different ways depending on their special needs and professional maturity.

South Carolina's new evaluation system makes reference to the importance of coaching for the first-year teachers. All first-year teachers are in an induction program and are mentored by an assistance team, which is expected to coach the first-year teachers.

But how are teams formed and how is coaching done? Teams in this program (known as Assisting, Developing, and Evaluating Professional Teaching, or ADEPT) consist of a district administrator, two principals or assistant principals, and an outside master teacher. This in South Carolina is the peer review team. As you can see, the persons comprising the team are not peers of the ordinary second-grade teacher or the ordinary tenth-grade biology teacher.

How is coaching done in this ADEPT system? By regulation, "coaching" is for first-year teachers only. The above-mentioned peer review team members observe each first-year teacher on separate occasions—as individuals, not as a team. The peer review team then meets and reaches consensus on its findings and recommendations. The team then calls in the teacher and hands down the recommendations. This is labeled "coaching" in the ADEPT evaluation system.

Peer review teams are advocated by the National Education Association and by many other state evaluation systems. You must ask, however: Is the team made up of *peers* or of administrators?

Are the teams true peers with the observed teacher and can their coaching be taken as teacher-to-teacher feedback and coaching, or is the peer review team an oxymoron for another outside administrative-supervisory evaluation? Do the words really mean what they say or is the jargon dressing up the same old evaluation-by-supervisor?

WHAT IS PEER COACHING?

Peer Coaching is a simple, nonthreatening structure designed for peers to help each other improve instruction or learning situations. The most common use is teacher-to-teacher peers working together on an almost daily basis to solve their own classroom problems. After becoming familiar with the simple five-step process, teachers can use their years of training from college and on the job to help each other solve classroom problems.

Have you ever coached or been coached in everyday life? How is it different from what traditionally happens in classrooms? Annie Sullivan taught Helen Keller to speak, but it was constant coaching that achieved the miracle. Even Olympic champion Mark Spitz, who won seven gold medals, received constant coaching on performance between winning his fifth and sixth medals. Name almost any famous artist, musician, writer, athlete, or performer—they have all sought and received coaching from fellow professionals. Michael Jordan, Jack Nicklaus, Mikhail Barishnikov, Leontyne Price, Arthur Ashe, and Brad Brown all received coaching on their performances.

These are examples of professionals seeking out coaching and advice on their professional performance. Given the importance of teaching, should not teaching be a profession where coaching and advice on performance in the classroom are actively sought and used? Just as gold medal winners use the simple routine of constant coaching to achieve excellence, classroom teachers and other professional educators in schools can use this simple, inexpensive process to improve performance. Peer Coaching is a simple, five-step framework designed for one professional educator to ask another professional to observe classroom performance in a nonjudgmental, nonevaluative way so that performance can improve. Properly used, Peer Coaching is a way to maximize all the money and time which has been spent on training, retraining, staff development, or skills enrichment. Peer Coaching allows a skill learned in training to be applied when the person returns to the workplace with no outside consultant to help him or her. Peer Coaching ensures the transfer of skills to the classroom where they will make a difference for students.

WHY DO IT?

While we may want to believe that there are no serious problems with public education, it would be naive of us to do so. Seldom in our history has public education received the volume and type of criticism it is receiving today. This criticism is coming from Democrats, Republicans, the wealthy, the poor, and all ethnic groups. The message is always the same: Public education is failing at its job. Often this criticism is accompanied by solutions such as privatization, vouchers, charter schools, and home schooling. If present trends continue, it is not unthinkable that public education as we know it will not exist fifty years from now.

Those who attack public education use data from sources such as TIMSS, SAT, and NAEP to point out how badly our schools are failing. The critics use these results to show that students from the United States do not compare favorably with their international counterparts and that they are not improving on internal tests such as the SAT.

Until recently, little of the criticism was focused on teachers. Now the critics have begun to point to the teaching profession as one of the causes of poor performance by American students. This type of attack is picking up momentum as many states begin to look at ways to improve the quality of their teaching force. In some extreme cases, there is talk of requiring teachers with existing teaching credentials to take an exam to prove they do not need remediation in order to continue teaching.

A report issued in 1996 by the Commission of Teaching and America's Future offers a glimpse of some of the problems surrounding the teaching profession. The commission found a profession that suffers from decades of neglect. It noted that reform of elementary and secondary education depends on the restructuring of its foundation, the teaching profession. The commission said restructuring must address the knowledge level of teachers and the redesign of schools to support high quality teaching.

One of the barriers identified by the commission as a hindrance to the development of a quality work force in public schools was lack of professional development and rewards for knowledge and skills. In addition to the lack of support for beginning teachers, most school districts invest little in ongoing professional development for experienced teachers and spend much of these limited resources on "hit-and-run" workshops. Further complicating this problem is the fact that most teachers have only three to five hours a week for planning purposes. This means there is almost no regular time in the school day for teachers to consult together about curriculum, instruction, and student matters.

Teaching under the best circumstances has always been a complicated, complex, and difficult task. A medieval curse uttered as a final condemnation said, "May you have to teach other people's children." Many of today's teachers are discovering the meaning of this curse. Teaching other people's children has become an extraordinarily difficult occupation, made no easier by other people who hold little confidence in what educators do and who constantly attack the educational system.

Although the commission's report, like other studies and reports, may overstate the case against public education, there can be no denying that public education has problem areas that must be corrected. One area that we must address is how to recruit the best-qualified people into education and how to keep them once they are in our system.

Peer Coaching is time-and cost-effective. Once teachers learn the structure, the process can become as routine and natural as coaching your child to ride a bike or to tie her shoelaces. Once practiced, internalized, and used regularly, it becomes a part of the daily routine. Peer Coaching is a formal outcomes-based structure to replace informal conversations concerning practice and classroom behaviors. Used properly, Peer Coaching is a powerful tool to produce internalization of a routine.

Peer Coaching should not be confused with a mentoring program which sets up an experienced person to guide or be a buddy to a new or inexperienced person. Mentors are valuable to every professional for problem solving, charting a career, and treading the political tightrope. They are important for new professional educators being inducted into teaching or principaling or training and for developing professional skills for incumbents who are traditionally isolated. Mentoring has a long and respectable history in the informal professional network and an even more promising future as more educators use mentors as part of the induction of new teachers.

The informal mentoring system has been used by professionals and politicians from Niccolò Machiavelli to the present. A neophyte is taken under the wing of a generous experienced professional to help him tread the corporate or political tightrope. Mentoring may be initiated by the incumbent or by the neophyte. The mentor provides connections, advice, consulting, and tips to the eager newcomer. The reward for the mentor is altruistic in helping the beginner to avoid the pitfalls and take advantage of the hard lessons and common mistakes. Informal mentoring arrangements are generally private, with mutual benefits to both parties. Promotion and loyalty are the two primary benefits.

Formal mentoring programs are more recent in education circles. Perhaps the best known mentoring program is Kettner's I/D/E/A Peer Assisted Leadership (PAL) program, in which groups of principals are set up under the leadership of a trained principal. Groups meet regularly to brainstorm and problem solve and may phone each other for more frequent advice. PAL functions both as a mentoring situation and as an informal study group for professional administrators.

WHO DOES IT?

This model for Peer Coaching was designed primarily for classroom teachers to observe, give feedback, and coach each other, one on one. The structure has five steps and simple rules to follow to keep the personal or judgmental aspects out of feedback and coaching. Teachers might think that this model can be used only with their best friend or a close professional coworker. In actuality, the structure and the safety net of rules allows even professionals who are not acquainted with each other to observe and coach. Although many initial reactions prompt participants in the training to say that this Peer Coaching is just like the old clinical supervision, further acquaintance with practice and daily use shows that it is not.

The motto for Peer Coaching is "No Praise, No Blame." The model also avoids feelings and personal reactions on the part of the coach so that he can merely report what exactly he observed concerning the teacher's request. The coach is almost like Sgt. Joe Friday in "Dragnet": "Just the facts, ma'am." With these Peer Coaching rules, the coach is not pressured to respond to the question "How did you *feel* the lesson went?" Since the model is nonjudgmental, only the requested observed data are shared until the teacher is ready, open, and willing to ask for suggestions for improvement.

In evaluative conferences with a supervisor, a teacher does not request the evaluator to observe a particular problem nor has she any choice about when or whether she wants to hear the recommendations for improvement from a supervisor who is no longer in the classroom. In this Peer Coaching model, the teacher requests help on a particular problem or a new skill she is trying to master. Therefore, after listening to the observed data in a factual manner, she can decide if true coaching is the next step and ask for the coach's suggestions for improvement.

With this "No Praise, No Blame" model, a teacher could theoretically use the structure with his worst enemy, his best friend, or a complete stranger—if they were both seeking the improvement of instruction and could set their egos and pride aside for that purpose.

Since the structure was designed primarily for solving classroom problems on an almost daily basis, the most common use is among teachers. During our years at the Department of Education in South Carolina, Dr. Jennings and I worked with teachers from 348 schools in the Effective Schools Program and an initial version of Peer Coaching. During my five years as the director for the South Carolina Center for the Advancement of Teaching and School Leadership, I brought Peer Coaching to the 150 Associate and Partner Schools in the restructuring reform in the state. We also brought the model to Maine school districts and to school principals in Hawaii for two years.

During my three years at Columbia College, I encouraged Peer Coaching among my education faculty as chair and associate chair. In John Goodlad's National Network for Educational Renewal, I used a form of Peer Coaching as we worked with arts and sciences departments, education departments, and professional development schools in sixteen colleges and universities across America.

Who uses it? One of the most effective uses of Peer Coaching has been among principals and staff development trainers. I always Peer Coach in a staff development seminar, using the same five steps and rules designed for classroom teachers.

Often, when leading a training session with a partner, one trainer can conduct the session while the other does Peer Coaching and real-time coaching at the back of the room. Taking notes for Peer Coaching is easy because the follow-up is after the seminar concludes. Real-time coaching involves the partner standing at the back of the room like a movie director, giving the slashing-throat sign for "Cut it short!" or urging "Speed Up!" during a boring segment. Real-time coaching requires trust and confidence in the coaching peer because the ego of the speaker is involved.

One of the most interesting Peer Coaching uses is to have a fellow principal coach her peer principal conducting a faculty meeting. Notice that the principals are peers, not a teacher coaching his boss or supervisor. Faculty meetings rapidly get more efficient when a peer principal is sitting at the back of the room taking notes for a Peer Coaching session. As a college professor and education department chair, I frequently had committee meetings, college classes, department meetings, and team meetings coached by a peer. If you think Peer Coaching is difficult to start among high school teachers, try it out on college professors!

Many other professionals use Peer Coaching almost unconsciously in their jobs. This Peer Coaching model seeks to formalize and to simplify that process into a simple, five-step structure which can be easily learned and used by any professional seeking to improve a situation. It is particularly effective, however, in the classroom and in staff development, formal presentations, and faculty meeting situations.

PURPOSES: PEER COACHING AND PEER REVIEW TEAMS

The hottest thing going now is the reform that revamps evaluation systems into peer review teams. These teams are recommended by the National Education Association and in South Carolina are written into the legislative mandates for teacher evaluation. After five years of pilot testing, the new evaluation system in the state (ADEPT) went into effect in the 1998–99 school year. The peer review teams will henceforth conduct evaluations for student teachers, provisional first-year teachers, annual contract teachers, and continuing contract teachers with tenure.

It is my belief that these peer review teams are neither peers nor really engaged in coaching. Teams are composed of district personnel, administrators, and master teachers who have been selected teachers-of-the-year. These are not peers for a given fourth-grade teacher or ninth-grade algebra teacher. Nor are they *teams* in the true sense of the word because they make separate observations of the teacher. The team does meet, reach consensus, and hand down recommendations to the teacher—or a pink slip—but there is not any coaching involved.

My experience and belief include progressive steps toward the effective use of peer review teams:

1. Change the culture of the school.
2. Use teambuilding and trust building to improve the environment.
3. Infuse Peer Coaching into the school.
4. Pursue other teambuilding processes such as Participatory Decision Making and Managing Change.
5. Keep supervisor evaluation for issues of termination.
6. Institute peer review teams after teachers are adept in using Peer Coaching.

Peer review teams will work in a school whose culture is characterized by teachers who work in teams, trust each other, and sincerely value internal professional growth. Peer review teams will not work in other cultures: they will still be state-mandated or central office–imposed evaluation by supervisors . . . by another name.

CHAPTER 2

Evaluation, Staff Development, and Peer Coaching

EVALUATION SYSTEMS: INSTRUCTIONAL IMPROVEMENT

What is the purpose of teacher evaluation systems? The words are simple and seem to mean exactly what they say: to evaluate teachers to see how well they are teaching. Good teachers are rewarded and instruction improves. Incompetent teachers are weeded out and instruction improves. Simple? Not exactly:

- Who evaluates teachers?
- By what standard is the evaluation done?
- At what point in a teacher's career is evaluation done?
- How often is a teacher evaluated?
- What are the results of evaluation?
- How does teacher evaluation improve instruction and increase the learning of students?

If we examine these two words—teacher evaluation—and this process in a detached, logic-only, Mr. Spock fashion, we find that it is indeed a simple process and one that should produce predictable results.

Who evaluates teachers? Principals evaluate teachers in the traditional school business model. At times, perhaps a supervisor such as a central office specialist or a curriculum specialist might evaluate teachers. The line of authority is clear.

By what standard is the evaluation done? This one is easy because state education departments have spent much time and many taxpayer dollars on the research and development of instruments to evaluate teachers. When I first went to South Carolina in 1984, the teacher evaluation instrument was a fifty-one-point minimalist checklist called Assessment for Performance in Teaching (APT), which awarded one point for "stating instructional goal" and one point for "show a sense of humor." During the years that the state mandated APT, fewer than 6 percent of teachers failed the APT. The year I left the state (1998) was the first year of implementation of the new, costly teacher evaluation system ADEPT (Assisting, Developing, and Evaluating Performance in Teaching). After three pilot years in districts and one year of implementation in teacher education departments (for student teachers), the ADEPT system with its peer review teams will now evaluate teachers in a more efficient and scientific manner.

At what point in a teacher's career is evaluation done? The standard template for evaluating teachers includes four points:

1. once as a student teacher waiting to be certified
2. once as a first-year teacher on the job
3. once a year for the first three years on the job
4. once every three years as a tenured teacher with a lifetime job

What are the results of evaluation? The evaluation form or report is placed in the teacher's personnel file and read again at the point of the next evaluation. If termination issues arise, the evaluation folder expands with other reports as the teacher brings court cases against the administration.

How does teacher evaluation improve instruction and increase the learning of students? Even from a detached, logical point of view, this question is difficult to answer. If the evaluation form or report is placed in the teacher's personnel file, how can the evaluation system help improve instruction? It can, you may argue, if the teacher is excellent, learns new skills, and constantly improves or keeps teaching at the same high level as new content is discovered or new tools such as computers or the Internet are improved. But what if the teacher is average or even incompetent? How will an evaluation report improve instruction in these cases?

At this point in the detached, logical analysis, we detect a breakdown because the results of evaluation often do not result in instructional improvement. Evaluation systems have not characteristically rewarded and motivated the excellent teachers nor have the systems weeded out the incompetent. If the teacher evaluation systems worked, we would have excellent teachers, no incompetents, and higher student test scores.

Let us return to *Who evaluates teachers?* Principals or supervisors with whatever area of expertise are usually taught how to supervise and evaluate the whole act of teaching. They may take one graduate course and/or have a week's training in how to use the new instrument; but, by and large, supervisor evaluation has been ineffective because of the internal politics of schools and districts and because of the largely impossible task of terminating an incompetent teacher without a lengthy court case.

By what standard is the evaluation done? With no disrespect intended toward research and development units who engage in the difficult process of meeting a state's mandates for teacher evaluation by designing a new instrument every decade, many teacher evaluation instruments do not improve instruction. The minimalist instruments, such as being sure each teacher can at least pass the National Teachers Examination (NTE) on general knowledge and the specialty area, or the APT whose points equate humor and instructional goals, have not improved the quality of teaching or instruction but they have assured us that beginning teachers know the absolute minimum. The absolute minimum may, however, be book learning or rote memory. An interesting instrument called DePict/DePart had the observer marking teacher behavior at thirty-second intervals on a checklist. After training in this method, some absolutely refused to use it as an evaluator and several excellent teachers departed the profession during the indignity of a hash mark every thirty seconds on selected behaviors.

At what point in a teacher's career is evaluation done? It is obvious that once-a-year evaluations done for student teachers, first-year teachers, and provisional teachers are not enough to help them improve instruction. Are we doing evaluation correctly or are we asking the wrong question? Are we doing the right thing to improve instruction? Evaluation does not improve instruction and seldom weeds out incompetent teachers, but Peer Coaching can.

How often is a teacher evaluated? Once-a-year evaluations probably cannot assist beginning and provisional teachers to improve instruction, but evaluations once every three years can do little to improve instruction among tenured teachers unless they are excellent. Many tenured teachers do learn new methods, master new skills and keep up with current content—but many do not. Evaluation every three years is not the key for improving instruction among tenured teachers.

What are the results of evaluation? Keeping evaluation results in a teacher's personnel file or using them to build a court case does not improve instruction. Evaluation should be formative or in process with teachers helping each other or seeking new skills through graduate courses or requested staff development. Teachers should and can help each other evaluate daily instruction as the experts and peers in the field. If the teacher requests Peer Coaching for a problem or new skill, if his peer assists him, then both teachers can improve instruction for their students. Peer Coaching can help teachers work on their everyday problems in pairs and seek outside help when their own experience and expertise are insufficient.

How does teacher evaluation improve instruction and increase the learning of students? The simple answer is that it does not, and seldom does it reward excellent teachers or weed out the incompetent. Why don't we take the money spent on teacher evaluation instruments and spend it on more worthwhile items such as:

1. a classroom telephone for every teacher
2. a computer for every teacher
3. a free graduate course or tech course for every teacher
4. a requested staff development model all teachers want
5. Peer Coaching

Instead of costly teacher evaluation instruments, research and development money could be spent on the "modest proposal" in chapter 12: making sure each student reads on grade level.

STAFF DEVELOPMENT: INSTRUCTIONAL IMPROVEMENT

What is staff development anyway? As a general rule, teachers have not been well prepared to serve the society that now exists, much less the society we are trying to create. We have tried for years to overcome the hurdle of inadequate teacher preparation in preservice by continually inservicing them. As John Goodlad says, the renewal of teacher education must go hand-in-hand with the restructuring of the schools for the twenty-first century. How many times have teachers gotten excited about new inservice programs or training but have had no support for it when they got back into the school? Therefore the new training ends up on the shelf in the closet or kept firmly in mind to implement when testing is over or after the spring break or next year. Yet those ideal conditions for implementation never happen. How many skeletons of the past training sessions would have made great impact on students had they been implemented?

What is real staff development? It begins with the assumption that professional teachers want to continually improve their skills and knowledge base. Let's look at other professions and the types and amounts of training these professionals receive.

Hairdressers attend seminars on how to cut and color hair once a month and frequently ask their peers to critique their work. A doctor cutting out tumors from a patient's body always has fellow professionals in the operating room for problem solving and diagnosis. Would you fly in a plane whose pilot did not have the latest training in wind shears and deicing?

IBM estimates that it spends ten to twelve days per year and 8–10 percent of its profit on training. Meanwhile most teachers spend three days on smorgasbord training and most school districts spend less than 1 percent of the total budget on training. Add to this fact that most teacher staff development takes place from 3 P.M. to 5 P.M., which is the worst possible dark hole of learning after an eight-hour workday. This time period makes it virtually impossible for even the best staff development training to get back to the classroom to help students. That is like asking a doctor to learn a new laser surgery technique after performing four hours in the operating room or asking a pilot to learn a new emergency landing procedure after flying through thunderstorms on both coasts. But we ask teachers to do it every day that we schedule inservice after school. Considering these circumstances, it is not surprising that more training is not transferred to the classroom where it makes an impact on the lives of students.

For years, we as educators have made certain assumptions about staff development. One is that if people like the training, they will use it in their classrooms. Characteristic workshop evaluations verify this assumption by asking: Did you enjoy the speaker? Was the topic relevant? Were the objectives met? Was it relevant to your work in schools? Were the lighting and seating arrangement conducive to learning? How good were the refreshments and lunch?

How many times do we give high marks on these evaluations? Trainers and researchers use the results to prove the training was effective. But, how much of it ever gets back in the classroom? The road is paved with good intentions. Nevertheless, back in the classroom, we find we don't have the skills and support to implement it, so it goes on the shelf. We then revert to the old way or search for a new bandwagon or a new panacea.

This brings to mind a story Will Rogers told about his advice to the military when Nazi submarines were becoming a threat in the Atlantic. Rogers told the audience that we should just heat the Atlantic Ocean to the boiling point: the subs would then pop up, and we could shoot them. The audience asked him how to heat the ocean water. Rogers replied that he had given them the solution and it was up to them to implement it. This is what we usually do to teachers with even the best staff development program. The real key and the point of Peer Coaching is what happens back in the classroom.

The second assumption is that if we liked the training and got an understanding of it, we would use it in the classroom. Trainers have assumed that knowledge of the skill automatically means that skills will transfer to the classroom. In graduate classes, we assume that if the professor talks about knowledge or skill and we demonstrate mastery on the skill, then we can use it in the classroom. That's the way we succeed in graduate school, but it doesn't work in the workplace. How many of those courses in which we got an A can we actually use in the classroom?

The third assumption is that if we could actually demonstrate the skill (perhaps in training conditions), then we would actually use it in classroom conditions. We find that in the trenches, conditions vary so much and the fires flare so often that what we demonstrated in the training session can't be done in the classroom because there is no ongoing coaching or support, on-site troubleshooting, or refreshers in the skill. Geb Runager at Marshall Elementary in Orangeburg, S.C. was tired of wasting money on staff development one-shots. He sent his fourth- grade teacher to Johns Hopkins University to become a trainer in Student Team Learning (STL). The teacher came back and trained the other teachers and is now the resident expert and troubleshooter. Runager spent the same amount of time and money as he would have to hire a national trainer who would have blown in, blown off, and blown out. The fourth grade teacher is always there for ongoing STL. Runager has now set aside time for teachers to coach each other to sustain old skills and learn new ones.

In a similar manner, while I was a college professor working with Professional Development Schools, I made efficient use of time and money by using a grant to train twelve public school teachers and five education faculty in Bernice McCarthy's 4 MAT Learning Styles. After three weeks of seminars, all the participants were able to return to their schools to be the in-house trainers for improving instruction by teaching all faculty the new skills of learning styles. The college professors used their skills to teach student teachers about learning styles. Of course, trainers worked in pairs and coached each other on their presentation and teaching skills.

Why have these assumptions been the obstacle for transfer of training or staff development or inservice directly to impact on student learning? Much of the reason for this problem has been our unwillingness to use all the elements for transfer of training. We know all we need to know about how training transfers, but we don't use those elements. If training is to impact on students, we must use the research on training. Preparation of student teachers could also benefit from this research on transfer of training so that teacher education could change from talking about a skill to following it through to transfer in the actual classroom setting.

Bruce Joyce and Beverly Showers, in their research on the coaching of teaching, have identified five elements that must be present in training if that training is to be transferred to the classroom so that it can impact on students:

- Theory
- Demonstration
- Practice
- Feedback
- Coaching

Theory is the rationale behind the skill or strategy and the principles that govern its use. It gives us a mental image of the skill and all the relevant research. It also provides us a framework for feedback and measurement. We get theory through readings, discussions, and lecture. The best example is the college classroom, where theory is endlessly expounded. This element is most common and is present in all training sessions. Typically this is the only element that exists in training sessions.

Demonstration means that the trainer simulates or models the skill. This allows the participant not only to hear about the skill but also to see the skill in action—under training conditions. This could take place in a setting similar to the workplace or in an unlike setting. It can take place while theory is presented or afterwards. It gives the participant the chance to view the skill through the eyes of the learner. It can be in person or on tape. Often people leave a session believing that if they saw the trainer demonstrate the skill, then they can do it. The disillusion comes when the person returns to the classroom and finds he still cannot perform the skill. We often forget that the trainer has done the skill hundreds of times, therefore in training conditions, the skill often seems easier to do than it is back in the classroom. Back in the classroom on Monday afternoon, this becomes apparent when the teacher attempts to apply the skill in the real world. When we suddenly realize that we need one more demonstration, there's no trainer around. Is this comparable to ordering the whiz bang slicer dicer on TV and not being able to assemble it when it arrives?

Practice in training involves guided practice in the presence of the trainer who has demonstrated the skill. Participants have a chance to practice the skill in training conditions. They practice with a partner or in a small group in a supposedly safe environment. The amount of practice depends on the complexity of the skill. The amount of practice needed to gain control of specific teaching practice depends on the complexity of the skills, and even simple ones take twenty to twenty-five practices, according to Joyce and Showers. In training conditions, how much of this is possible? How many practices does each individual actually have within the training session?

Feedback is giving information about a skill once it has been performed. Again, it is the "Dragnet" component: "Just the facts, ma'am!" and nothing but the facts. To be effective, feedback must be specific. Feedback can be given while the skill is being performed or later. Feedback is nonevaluative because it is simply a replay of the facts. When giving feedback, a person is simply a camcorder, replaying what actually happened: no praise, no blame, no evaluation.

Training has included all four of these elements, but with all four present, there is still a low percentage of transfer. By looking at the table below, we can see that the number of people who can learn or acquire a skill goes from low to high with each added element, but the number who can apply it remains low even with all four of these elements present in training.

	Acquire	Apply
Theory	low	very low
Demonstration	medium	very low
Practice	high	low
Feedback	high	low

The fifth element that raises the acquire and apply ratios is *coaching*. When coaching is added to the four elements, application rates take a sharp turn upward. Coaching is more than feedback (a replay of the facts) and takes place once the teacher is back in the classroom setting. Coaching assumes that the teacher is ready to move beyond feedback suggestions, possibilities, planning sessions, watching a master lesson, and mutual learning. What do you do when your job requires you to transfer a learned skill such as some in industry? Joyce and Showers found that on-the-job follow-up never ended and was continuous.

When we add the essential element of coaching, we find that a high number acquire the skill and can apply it in the workplace. With this jump in rates, it makes no sense not to add this element. All teachers need to transfer new skills into active repertoire where on-site practice and feedback and coaching occurs. If we don't add this fifth element, all training money, time, and effort is down the drain.

Chart 1. Does Staff Development Training Transfer to Actual Practice?

5%	of learners will transfer a new skill into their practice as a result of theory
10%	will transfer a new skill into their practice with theory and demonstration
20%	will transfer a new skill into their practice with theory, demonstration, and practice within the training
25%	will transfer a new skill into their own use with theory, demonstration, practice within the training, and feedback
90%	will transfer a new skill into use with theory, demonstration, practice, feedback, and coaching

Source: Dr. Bruce Joyce, "Staff Development Awareness Conference," Columbia, S.C., January 1987.

Why should any professional engage in Peer Coaching to improve performance? Joyce and Showers can give a researched answer to the question, shown in chart 1. When teachers attend a staff development training session to learn a new skill and hear only *theory,* only 5 percent will transfer that new skill into their teaching back at the workplace. Hearing only theory means "sit and git," like many of us did throughout college and graduate school. The expert with his captive audience talks at great length about the new skill while the listeners are expected to take notes and be able to apply the skill. Many high school, middle school, and even elementary school students are in the "sit and git" mode, except they are also expected to regurgitate the notes they take from the lecture back into something we call tests. The only difference between many staff development workshops and a lecture course is that persons who attend training sessions seldom take a test or have opportunities for supported application of the new skills.

Joyce and Showers's second finding was that 10 percent will transfer new skills into everyday practice with theory *and a good demonstration* on the part of the trainer. The percentage is doubled if in addition to talking about the new idea or new skill, the trainer can show how to do it. As a soccer coach, I can talk about headers; but until I show the team how to do it, the theory is worthless. If the training session is on active audience participation, the trainer must be able to show how to do it as well as talk about it. But still, with theory and a good demonstration, there is only a 10 percent transfer of new skills.

The transfer percentage rises to 20 percent if the staff development session includes theory, a good demonstration, *and practice.* Practice at the training session itself is what doubles the transfer rate. Practice under the guidance and with the support of the trainer has many implications for time and grouping in staff development sessions. Practice does not mean one or two people coming to the front to experience the skill for the whole group. It means dividing the audience into small groups, supplying time and materials, and letting everyone try the new skill. Guided practice during the training session is quite different from sending participants out with only theory and one demonstration to practice back in the workplace. The 20 percent transfer rate is dependent on practice in the session itself.

The rate of transfer goes up to 25 percent if *feedback* is added to theory, demonstration, and practice. Feedback means reflective shadowing or being the extra set of eyes and ears to reflect back just as a mirror would. Feedback is similar to being a camera with no evaluation, no judgment, no suggestions for improvement—"Just the facts, ma'm" as Joe Friday used to say on Dragnet.

The crucial element, according to Joyce and Showers, is *coaching*. Coaching, added to theory, demonstration, practice, and feedback, increases the transfer of new skills to 90 percent. That numerical jump alone should be enough to get professionals to try coaching. Even if the numbers jumped to only 50 percent, it would be worth investing time in a structured model to coach.

If we look realistically at most training programs on which we are spending thousands of dollars, most include only theory and demonstration with perhaps some token practice. Almost none include feedback, much less coaching on a regular, systematic basis. Many packaged staff development models do have feedback and coaching as a part of their list of implementation requirements, but they do not describe how to do Peer Coaching itself. Neither do these models allow for the time required to train observers and the frequency of their observations in schools. Outside observers are fine if they can observe almost daily to give teachers the support they need to practice a new skill. Until schools have trained observers, however, we can use Peer Coaching.

One school spent $23,000 for a staff development program, but the participants got feedback and coaching only once every six months on a new skill they were expected to use on a daily basis. It is true that the coaches had to be intensively trained, but Peer Coaching could have helped the rate of transfer by providing daily feedback and coaching, professional to professional.

We must remember that teaching is a very complex skill that requires not only periodic updating and retraining but must also include some internal support system. This support system should allow teachers daily refinement of skills. Peer Coaching is a system that will allow almost daily coaching. As with other professionals, teachers must have routine training, coaching, performance, then more coaching. It is impossible to do this if teachers have to wait until the January staff development days.

PEER COACHING: INSTRUCTIONAL IMPROVEMENT

Our staff development has been the one-shot deal which does not include on-site, continual coaching and refresher courses in skills. If teaching is to develop into a true profession, the training must include elements to transfer skills to the classroom. The time and money that other professions devote to training must become characteristic of the teaching profession. The complexity of teaching—which is both a science and an art—requires more than after-school lectures to develop a true professional. Who would want a doctor who has been trained only with the *theory* of appendix removal or a pilot who has only seen a *demonstration* of wing deicing or a hairdresser who has only *practiced* coloring hair once in training? We will, however, train teachers after school with no on-site follow-up or feedback and coaching and expect to produce thinking citizens in a thriving democracy. It just won't happen! Training teachers to make those synapses fire in the brains of learners is just as important as training doctors to remove tumors that block those synapses.

Beverly Showers conducted an experiment on the effects coaching has on transfer. All the teachers in the study received three months of training in a specific skill. Half the group also received coaching back at the school site as they implemented the skill. The other half did not receive the coaching. Results show that 75 percent of those who received coaching transferred the skill appropriately to the classroom. In the group that was not coached, only 15 percent transferred it to the classroom. Many of the teachers who did not receive coaching delayed using the skill and after approximately six months had lost the skill entirely.

The purpose of Peer Coaching is to provide for the transfer of training elements in an everyday situation so that teachers can manage them. Peer Coaching is not content, but rather a process that can be used for any skill. Its major purpose is to help implement new training or help sustain existing training so that the training will impact on student learning in the classroom. Peer Coaching ensures that theory, demonstration, practice, feedback, and coaching transfer any training from the lecture room to the classroom with ongoing troubleshooting and renewal.

The present model of Peer Coaching involves some direct advantages and indirect advantages over more = traditional clinical supervision models. It is not intended as a model for either supervision or evaluation. This model is directly as the name states: Peer = between peer professionals on the same level, Coaching = short informal observations on one specific, teacher-identified area. This model to be used between professionals on the same level is not intended for evaluation nor to set up one as the master teacher. It is coaching in the best sense, perhaps as athletic coaches do in certain phases of their work. It is intended to be brief, time-saving, and effective.

Our contention is that one-shot staff development does not improve instruction and increase student learning unless it "takes" in a school—unless the new teaching skill becomes part of the daily routine. We believe that the way to make any new staff development "take" in a school is either to keep the consultant on call or to use Peer Coaching. Teachers using Peer Coaching can assist each other with observation, feedback, and coaching on any specific skill in the new staff development model.

For instance, if the head of the science department in a middle school is having difficulty with including Type Four learners in earth science, her peer coach (who has also been trained in 4 MAT Learning Styles, Excel Corp.) could observe and give feedback on specific opportunities to include learning activities that appeal to Type Four learners. In fact, this scenario played out in one of our Professional Development Schools in Columbia.

The author has worked as teacher, principal, state department consultant, training consultant, and presenter. With my additional experience as a statewide restructuring center director and college professor, I have been trained in the whole alphabet soup of staff development models. Some of the staff development models have been great and some have been useless. The great models like 4 MAT and EST can and have been used with Peer Coaching to infuse them into the school culture and into the daily routine of teaching. Only when this happens with whatever effective and/or expensive staff development model can the model improve instruction. Even the best teaching methods brought in by a consultant cannot improve instruction unless the professionals in a school help each other—with Peer Coaching or some other method—to incorporate the new methods into daily routine for the improvement of instruction.

This fact of teaching life is why we can predict the eventual failure of any new program or school reform that is not routinized into a teacher's daily repertoire. Peer Coaching helps bring well-researched staff development models into the school culture because teachers are on the spot to assist their peers. All one must do to start the Peer Coaching process is to request a visit from another teacher to observe, give feedback, and coach.

CHAPTER 3
Learning about Peer Coaching

BACKGROUND

Peer Coaching is not a clinical supervision program in which a group of highly skilled supervisors provide observation, feedback, and evaluation to persons who are not their peers. As originally conceived by Morris Cogan with the Harvard/Newton summer school in 1973, a group of supervisors from the school of education and the school district were trained in specific procedures designed to improve instruction. Both neophytes and experienced teachers were the subjects in clinical supervision. In general, five formal procedures were set up: pre-observation conference, observation, conference planning, post-observation conference, and process review. Each step took almost an hour and the formal observation was set for an entire class period. Usually neither the pre-observation conference nor the post-observation conference took place on the same day as the observation, simply because of the amount of time involved.

In the pre-observation conference, the supervisor and the teacher to be observed planned the lesson to be observed. The supervisor had an improvement agenda to follow for observation and eventual evaluation and she also made suggestions in planning the lesson. The teacher followed the supervisor's lead in this first step. The observation was script taped in its entirety, with all elements of the lesson observed and noted for a full hour. In the conference planning, the formal script tape was examined and categorized for certain prescribed elements. The supervisor planned a script for the conference and kept evaluation in mind as the end product along with the improvement of instruction. With the supervisor again as the leader, the teacher listened to the scripted agenda and participated according to the excellence of the lesson. The process review listed the chosen procedures for improvement.

In general, the time involved was a minimum of five hours over two to five days, with at times a lapse of a week between observation and conference. In certain forms of clinical supervision, a team of up to eight persons planned, observed and conferenced an individual teacher.

Etymology—word origins—is always an interesting aspect of an explanation of the terms supervision, evaluation, peer, and coaching. As a graduate professor teaching courses in supervision and evaluation, I can attest that few if any of the graduate students in a supervision and evaluation course ever looked at the meanings of the two parts of the word "supervision." "Vision" can mean far-seeing, and "super" is Latin for superior or above. It is an exciting word, supervision: one who sits above and is far seeing. We educators have managed to bowdlerize that beautiful version into almost a dirty word these days.

In an impressive analysis of the present state of supervision, Wendy Poole (1994) compares the evolution of supervision with the family trees of neo-traditionalism and neo-progressivism. Poole uses the Darling-Hammond and Sclan contrast. Linda Darling-Hammond and Eileen Sclan (1992) define the neo-traditionalist branch as located within the tradition of behavioral psychology, those who view teaching as the technical process of applying scientific knowledge:

> Neo-traditionalists are concerned with specifying and producing teacher behaviors thought to be associated with learning. . . . The goal is to coach teachers to display these behaviors rather than to identify and solve actual problems of practice.

Neo-traditionalists find a convenient research-based set of criteria for judging the competence of teachers. Usually this hierarchical set of criteria can be restructured into a training module and an evaluation checklist so that administrators can evaluate teachers on the basis of their ability to demonstrate the chosen teaching criteria. Madeline Hunter's Theory into Practice reforms for effective teaching were adopted by South Carolina into a series of training modules and eventually into an evaluation checklist. Hunter herself (at SDE PET conferences in 1988 and 1989) denounced the transmogrification of her effective teaching theories and practices into an hierarchical evaluation checklist. Many of her wonderful theories and directions for effective teaching were changed into a rigid training model whose end result was to produce teachers who could display the behaviors Hunter recommended, leaving much of the artistry out of the art and science of teaching.

However, despite Hunter's protests about the state's PET version of her research and practice, it was and is a better instructional model than any formerly used by teachers.

Darling-Hammond and Sclan (1992) contrast the neo-progressive branch as one which is located within the tradition of cognitive development. Adherents of this branch view teaching as a complex and uncertain process requiring continuous judgment and decision making on the part of the teacher. The neo-progressive would focus on the collegial and professional aspects of supervision. The present model of Peer Coaching grows further along this branch of evolutionary progress.

Both neo-traditionalists and neo-progressives focus on the term *clinical supervision* as practiced by Cogan and Goldhammer. While neo-progressivism has focused on the reflective, on the job aspect of the original clinical supervision, neo-traditionalism has perhaps a better claim to clinical supervision as a term. I support their claim. Supervision no longer means a far-seeing one who sits above, if it ever did. In many cases, supervision is now the dirty word which promulgates the class consciousness of superior administrators or evaluators who sit above inferior classroom teachers and claim to know better than they do. Supervisors expect teachers to learn a chosen model of effective teaching and reproduce the chosen behaviors. Their evaluation ratings are based on the teachers' ability to reproduce those chosen behaviors. Supervisors, in this instance, include administrators and master teachers who are released from the classroom to perform administrative duties such as serving on ADEPT peer review teams, whose members are not peers, but supervisors in another guise. It is supervision by committee instead of by an individual principal.

The clinical part of clinical supervision indicates that it takes place in the clinic or classroom where the science of teaching is performed. Clinical supervision sounds great and in many instances is. But expecting teachers to reproduce researched behavioral criteria in the ordinary classroom leaves out all of the current research on how the brain learns (e.g., Renata and Geoffrey Caine's 1994 *Making Connections: Teaching and the Human Brain*) and teaching to different learning styles (e.g., Bernice McCarthy's 1996 *About Learning*)

In the sense that neo-progressives view supervision as assisting teachers and students to construct meaning out of their daily interactions concerning teaching and learning, Peer Coaching also falls within this branch. In learning theory, this view could also be termed constructivism. At this point, however, I depart from supervision altogether and advocate a waiting period for peer review teams until the culture of schools and teaching is transformed into a professional collegial atmosphere of problem-solving professionals who observe, give feedback, and coach each other in the improvement of teaching and learning.

If Peer Coaching is implemented, school culture can change. Or as school culture changes with the professional educators building trust, teams, and a commitment to instructional improvement from within, Peer Coaching can be the mechanism for peer review teams and real evaluation systems to succeed. In such a school culture, real peer review teams could succeed. Until then they are only another name for administrative supervision and evaluation. Peer review teams do produce enormous budgets for research and development specialists and for the administrators who administer the resulting evaluation instrument.

This Peer Coaching model is a reflective model which differs from both mentoring programs and clinical supervision. In this model, the word "peer" has its real meaning: coaching occurs between professionals of equal status. Mentoring usually denotes that one of the parties is more experienced or knowledgeable. Clinical supervision implies that there is a supervisor and that evaluation is involved. This model of Peer Coaching also differs from other models which include evaluation or set-up second-line supervisors as coaches who evaluate. With a supervisor who evaluates, the teachers have no choice about time, technique, or suggestions for improvement. In this reflective model, the teacher chooses the time, what he or she wants to improve, and the coaching situation. There is a greater chance that improvement will occur if the situation is self-imposed, that is, if the teacher makes the request for coaching herself.

Peer Coaching, however, has not been confined to the classroom, although it started as a teacher-to-teacher device. It was used immediately as trainer-to-trainer coaching, including real-time coaching where one trainer would stand at the back of the room with throat-slashing, hand-napping, or speed-up signs in real time as another led the staff development session. Or vice versa! It has also been used for principal-to-principal coaching when principals led faculty meetings into a less-boring routine.

From 1990 to 1995, the state legislature in South Carolina funded a restructuring center for schools and colleges, the South Carolina Center for the Advancement of Teaching and School Leadership. The Center brought the EIA reform act to full fruition by training teachers to take leadership roles in changing schools or to be proactive participants on change teams with parents, administrators, community members, and college faculty. For all the staff development and leadership seminars which it designed and conducted, the Center used Peer Coaching to assist the participants in learning the new techniques. Then it taught them the simple, five-step model of Peer Coaching in order that they might use it for teams back at the workplace. The model provided follow-up and implementation strategies for other staff development and leadership programs that were instituted for teams to improve teaching and schools as well as community or school, meetings.

Peer Coaching was used for Center-designed and-implemented programs such as Managing Change, Utilizing Test Scores to Change Teaching, the Strength Deployment Inventory, 4 MAT Learning Styles, Deming's Total Quality Management as it was adapted for schools as Total Quality Education, E-Mail and the Internet, Teambuilding, and others.

When the state legislature cut the funding for the innovative state restructuring center in 1995, my colleagues and I took Peer Coaching to other media. The twelve Regional Fellows whom we had trained at the Center to become staff development leaders in their own areas spread Peer Coaching as they implemented other programs with teachers in their own schools and districts. I became the head of a college education department, while Dr. James Jennings left the state department to become a district superintendent in the northwestern corner of the state. One Center trainer took Peer Coaching to the high school where he became assistant principal and staff developer. Others took it to banking and to a college's Professional Development Schools.

At that juncture in time, 1995, Peer Coaching had many applications in schools and community groups. In the following years, all of these applications were explored, personalized, refined, re-examined, and institutionalized as use increased and adaptations were used locally, regionally, and nationally.

CHANGING SCHOOL CULTURE:
THE THREE PHASES OF PEER COACHING

One avenue of improving the quality of teachers is to provide a culture in which teachers are expected to interact with each other to discuss their vocation. This type of collegial culture would do much to improve the quality of instruction that goes on in our schools.

Teachers need the opportunity to have conversations with other teachers regarding teaching and learning. They need to observe others engaged in the practice of teaching. And teachers should have the opportunity to have peers observe them practicing their profession and to give them feedback about what they see. Peer Coaching is one way to introduce this type of culture into a school.

Everyone can profit from having a coach. Unfortunately, in the teaching profession, we only think of the term "coach" as it relates to athletics. This is not true with other professions. In fact, one does not have to look far to find other professions that use coaching by peers as a means of improving performance or improving the chances for success: law, medicine, athletics, cosmetology, and architecture are just a few of the fields that practice this type of coaching. A football coach does not hesitate to ask questions of another coach or to visit to learn more about his profession. He would even ask fellow coaches to give him feedback regarding his performance as a coach and to offer suggestions on how he might improve. The same attitude is seen in a school district's attorney, who does not hesitate to go to his partners for feedback or to discuss a particularly difficult case.

We must insist that educators have the same type of attitude when it comes to teaching and learning. We must expect this type of behavior. Teachers must grow professionally every year they are in the classroom. This expectation must be coupled with a culture that not only expects this type of behavior but also provides the type of school organization and structure that allows it. Peer Coaching will not occur by itself. It must have an advocate in a position to make it happen. Peer Coaching can make a difference in your teaching staff.

The Three Phases: Steps to Building Trust and Changing School Culture

Although true Peer Coaching is voluntary on the part of professional teachers, the initial stages must be carefully orchestrated and structured for it ever to become institutionalized in a school. Teachers and principals have so many other responsibilities that a careful schedule of gradual indoctrination into the professional advantages of using Peer Coaching is necessary. If the initial stages of Peer Coaching are offered as the usual one day of training or staff development and used on a voluntary basis, it will go up on the dusty shelf with so many other innovative techniques that have not been carefully nurtured.

From my experience, I have found that it is necessary to phase-in Peer Coaching in order to carry teachers from a formal structure where teachers are required to participate to a teacher-controlled process of professionals helping each other on a voluntary basis. The three phases are:

1. Peer Watching
2. Peer Feedback
3. Peer Coaching

Peer Watching is designed to move teachers from the traditional isolation into a more collegial relationship of visiting the classrooms of other professionals. This phase is to break down the barriers that have built up through years of isolation. These barriers have been reinforced by evaluation procedures and even incentive programs that have put teachers in competition with each other. If you are competing for money or merit raises, you are reluctant to share innovative ideas or practices. Because these norms are well entrenched, this phase of Peer Watching is vital in the traditional school organization. It is also necessary to get teachers to feel comfortable about visiting in another teacher's classroom without feeling like an intruder.

Teachers have not normally visited and observed for any reason so this is a great barrier to overcome within the normal routine of the traditional school. Other professionals feel at ease watching peers. They have it built into early training and practice, but teachers have had to learn by listening to education professors instead of watching master teachers. In order to get teachers accustomed to observing each other, it is necessary to begin true Peer Coaching with Peer Watching. Peer Watching overcomes these obstacles by making it easier on the teacher visited and the visiting teacher. The purpose is to increase the comfort zone.

Peer Watching is just that: watching and nothing else—no comments and no exchange of information. Teachers can, however, begin honing their observation skills by practicing taking notes or by simply writing down the objective of the lesson. Neither teacher should talk or comment to the other about the lesson during the Peer Watching phase. Watching is merely observing. This is where the No Praise, No Blame motto takes effect. Peer Watching requires no interaction between teacher and watcher.

The only exchange necessary is for teams of teachers to decide on a weekly focus for Peer Watching. For example, all watchers might look for lesson closure one week and lesson focus the next. Groups of teachers should meet as a study group to exchange ideas on Peer Watching: how each felt as watcher and watchee and how their professionalism has evolved as the comfort zone has increased. Discussion groups are necessary in order to decide when the group is ready to move from Peer Watching to Peer Feedback. Time spent on Peer Watching will vary from school to school. I recommend at least two months in this Peer Watching phase. The time could vary depending on the readiness of teachers to receive feedback from other professionals outside the evaluation cycle.

The next phase is Peer Feedback and it is designed as a transition between merely watching and true coaching. Peer Feedback involves the Request, the Visit, the Coach's Review of the notes, the Talk after the Visit, and the Process Review. The only difference between Peer Feedback and Peer Coaching comes in the Talk after the Visit. After the data are collected, the only job the coach has in Peer Feedback is to present the data gathered. The motto here is Joe Friday's "Just the facts, ma'am." Nothing else. The one who observes and gives feedback is just a mirror of what went on in the classroom. No coaching or suggestions for improvement take place during this phase.

This offers teachers a chance to practice the logistical skills of feedback for a period of about two months. Note-taking skills can be refined and the observer can begin to feel more comfortable. Teachers can experiment with many data-gathering devices. Observers can hone their observation skills and learn to focus on one concern, not on everything that goes on in a classroom. They can also practice restraining themselves from evaluative comments. This is a time when those who give feedback can experiment with varying lengths of observation.

Since teachers begin to select the skills they want coaches to observe, they are forced to focus on the teaching act in ways they have never done before. By eliminating suggestions or true coaching from this phase, teachers feel more comfortable with the Request and Talk steps. By allowing these two months for practice on feedback, teachers become more comfortable when they reach the true Peer Coaching phase. Depending on the readiness level of the teachers and their willingness to offer suggestions in a professional manner, the group can move on to true Peer Coaching. This decision should be made by teams of teachers or group shared decision making.

The final phase of Peer Coaching is true coaching. The only difference between Peer Feedback and Peer Coaching is that the coach plans and offers suggestions for improvement if the teacher indicates willingness to be coached. After gathering the data, the coach reviews the notes and lists three possibilities for improvement. He has these ready during the Talk after the Visit if the teacher asks for them.

True Peer Coaching is done in five simple steps. It is easier to phase-in peer coaching if teachers adhere to the rules and structure defined in the following chapters. As the model is internalized, coaches and teachers deviate from the rules and adapt the model as they need it.

WHAT DOES IT LOOK LIKE?

The entire process of this model of Peer Coaching can take from forty to sixty minutes from start to finish. It is clearly intended to take place within the limits of one working day. The terminology is user-or teacher-friendly and is intended to imply informal collegiality. Instead of using the words conference and observation, the five steps are labeled:

1. The Teacher Requests a Visit
2. The Visit
3. The Coach Reviews the Notes and Lists Some Possibilities
4. The Talk after the Visit
5. The Review of the Process

The whole psychological mind-set of this user-friendly model is different from evaluative models. Instead of the supervisor scheduling a visit, pairs of teachers working together know that they are in this for the purpose of helping each other improve instruction and the teaching/learning situation for children on an almost daily, neighborly, professional basis.

Therefore, the first step is in the teacher's hands: the teacher requests a Visit. The Visit may be to observe one specific point of instruction or classroom management in which the teacher needs help. Or it may simply be for her peer to observe a new technique the teacher wants to try. The teacher requests that her peer come into the classroom for a limited period. This saves release time, prescheduling, and the delayed formality of evaluation observations. Because requested Visits are for one specific point instead of a whole lesson and because they can take place in as few as ten minutes, this model of Peer Coaching can occur almost daily and can be totally nonthreatening, like the informality of doctors sitting in on each other's operations. With these informal exchanges characteristic of other true professions, from musicians to medical doctors, teacher professionalism can improve.

The Visit is also different from the formal observation in that both parties know that it is a professional peer exchange: no evaluation, no supervising—just a friendly "help me" visit. Since the visit is nonevaluative and the teacher has requested feedback on one specific area, there are no surprises nor wholesale and sometimes unwanted feedback of everything that went on. In other words, the teacher knows what to expect: feedback on the Request, no extras. It also makes the Visit easier on the coach: one request to fulfill and ten minutes out of his teaching day to help a fellow professional who can later do the same thing for him.

The Coach's Review of her notes is also user-friendly because the notes have one focus, instead of a cover-the-waterfront hour-long observation. One focus means that one item is charted, script taped, or otherwise recorded for feedback. If the coach and her peer are familiar enough with this model of Peer Coaching, then the coach can also list coaching suggestions if the peer is ready for them after the feedback. Technically in the first stages of Peer Coaching, the coach merely feeds back exactly what she saw on the item requested. When the peer is ready, he asks for suggestions for improvement or real Peer Coaching. The point is sound psychologically: the teacher *requests* a Visit, the teacher gets feedback on an item and *requests* coaching for improvement after the feedback. In other words, the proactive responsibility is always in the teacher's court. He is not the passive recipient of supervisory evaluation as in some clinical supervision.

The Talk after the Visit is also different from the post-observation conference of clinical supervision. The teacher knows that there will be no evaluation, no blame, and no praise: merely a professional exchange where he will get honest feedback on what happened in the teaching/learning situation on the one item of instruction or management that he himself requested. *If* he is ready, he will get some coaching and suggestions for improvement on the one item, not from a supervisor or a superior teacher, but from the professional peer whom he asked to visit his classroom.

The Process Review in this model of Peer Coaching does not determine evaluation: it merely reviews the Peer Coaching rules and, one hopes, continues the cycle of friendly professional Peer Coaching by setting up another coaching Visit or a new Visit where the peer becomes the coach for her fellow teacher.

Peer Coaching models are in use in several states with the title "peer coaching." They are in reality second-line supervisors called peer coaches, but the meaning of the word "peer" has been obliterated.

In true Peer Coaching, peers coach each other. A peer is a person who is on the same level as the coach. Peer Coaching for professionals implies that two persons are on the same level, although they may have varying degrees of skills in certain areas. One strength may balance another area of need. Both persons may have gone through the same workshop or training to learn new skills and by coaching each other, both became better. If businesses had time and money to retain a consultant who does a new skill workshop to come back into the workplace one-on-one as the employees try new skills, Peer Coaching would not be necessary. However, few businesses or schools have that kind of time or money. Until that idealistic day, Peer Coaching must have a place in our classrooms and schools.

Who are the professionals who already engage in formal or informal Peer Coaching in order to improve performance? Performers such as dancers, musicians, athletes, singers, and artists ask for and get coaching from their peers as well as from their trainers. Hair stylists such as those in Chong's International Salon frequently pull out a strand and ask another operator's opinion on color intensity or timing. Chong does not consider it demeaning to ask the opinion of a fellow professional. This Peer Coaching does not replace the monthly workshops she attends to upgrade her coloring, cutting, and curling skills.

What other professionals freely ask for coaching? High school football coaches such as Buddy Jennings had many peers among high school and college ranks. When a new offensive play devastated his team one Friday night, Coach Jennings immediately called Dick Sheridan and other coaches—peers—to get some advice on how to set up a new defense and to change his coaching strategies before the next Friday. His job depended on winning high school football games, so asking a peer for help was not demeaning to him as a professional.

Which professionals do not regularly ask their peers for help? Teachers, principals, managers, mid-level trainers, superintendents, speech-makers, report-readers, committee members, school board members, Sunday School teachers, Chamber of Commerce members. Why? In education as well as in some business operations, it has been considered dangerous to expose performance to others who have similar jobs because ideas or innovations might be diminished if peers (not subordinates) see them in use. In traditional operations such as schools, the isolation and tenure is a guarantee for job security. Any adult who observes has been regarded as an evaluator.

At the end of the nineteenth century, teachers were isolated in one-room schoolhouses, interacting only with subordinates (student), with occasional visits from superiors (evaluators). At the end of the twentieth century, most teachers are still isolated in one-room schoolhouses connected by a common parking lot. Today we call them classrooms in consolidated school building, but the philosophical and physical isolation is much the same—"caves" as Roland Barth's teacher names them. Because of this setting, many teeachers have developed the attitudes of "Just give me my studens and let me close the door and teach them."

This practice of isolation no longer works for our country and even less for our school rooms.

The same could be said for other operations in which isolation is not productive. Companies typically spend 8 to 10 percent of the budget on training or staff development. The manager who has learned the new skill or new method returns to work with her subordinates and may have great incentive to apply the skill. In isolation or with traditional authoritarian methods, the new skills may die a slow death. With Peer Coaching, however, the manager would feel free to call in a peer who went to the same training or another respected peer to give her feedback and coaching on obstacles to fully applying the new skill as she does her job.

Do principals, managers, speakers, superintendents, or mid-level trainers get coaching? The excellent ones do. Peer Coaching for principals has been part of the South Carolina Effective Schools Training program since 1986. After a module of training and a strategy session, an improving principal would carry out the practice in a faculty meeting. The consultant or a district trainer or a fellow principal would observe the principal making the presentation or leading the discussion and then give feedback and coaching. Peer Coaching was developed as the final module of training in that year-long intensive program. Many principals saw it not only as a benefit in teacher-to-teacher coaching, but also as support for their own professional growth in the jungle of mandates and regulations for administrators.

Who else can benefit from Peer Coaching? Salespersons or administrators or managers trying to sell an idea or program to an audience can improve performance by having a peer professional observe and coach. The director of West Coast direct sales for a major Internet company certainly receives coaching as he exhorts his staff to sell more space. Imagine the benefits of a fellow superintendent observing while the superintendent persuades the school board to invest in new curriculum and then providing coaching on improving performance for the next meeting. Trainers who lead workshops for small or large groups find that a peer trainer who provides coaching on particular aspects of the three-hour or three-day session is as invaluable to training as are clear handouts, visuals, and refreshments. Timing for topics, audience reaction and participation, and body language are areas in which trainers seek Peer Coaching. As soon as I began to train people using this structured model I developed, I have never been without a peer coach for any training session or presentation.

As the level of trust between peers develops and each becomes skilled in using Peer Coaching, real-time coaching can help in the same way that directors guide live or on-camera performances of actors and newscasters. A real-time peer coach standing at the back of the room can give hand signals so that the speaker will speed up, take a break, speak louder, get the audience involved now, move around, or slow down. Real-time coaching works best when the peers involved are also co-trainers. The ideal pairing has one coaching while the other is speaking and keeps them both highly invested in the flow of the presentation.

ROLES

The teacher's role in Peer Coaching also begins with a commitment. This often depends on the job the principal did in selling Peer Coaching to the faculty. Teachers must be willing to develop a common language so that feedback will hang on the specific science of teaching. Feedback and coaching depend on a common vocabulary, and Peer Coaching promotes the science of teaching to discuss the terminology.

The role of the teacher is to be open-minded and to be interested in finding new and better ways to conduct school business. Excellent teachers have always looked for better ways to do classroom business. Other teachers have to realize that looking for another way is not admitting weakness, but merely seeking a wider range of skills to better serve students. Finally, teachers must be willing to share adult needs: to talk and communicate with adults during the working day.

Role of the Teacher

The teacher must:

1. commit to Peer Coaching to analyze and improve instruction.
2. be willing to develop and use a common language of collaboration in order to discuss the total teaching act without praise or blame.
3. be like Chaucer's clerke—gladly would he learn and gladly teach—to request observation and to observe as coach when requested.
4. be open-minded and willing to look for better ways of conducting classroom business. Excellent teachers always stretch beyond what they do now toward new learning to improve instruction.
5. act as a colleague and as a professional.

What are the outcomes of Peer Coaching and what can it do for a school or a group of professionals? First, it can establish a line of communication between faculty members by providing a safe framework for discussing instructional issues. It provides teachers a chance to think and talk about their lessons, to examine their lessons in detail and bring to a conscious level what many of us do instinctively. It allows teachers to expand teaching skills by expanding coaching skills. Teachers often learn more in the role of coach than they do as a peer being coached. Many valuable teaching skills are automatically shared as teachers coach each other almost daily. It provides adult and professional companionship to teachers who have been closeted with children in the traditional structure.

Part of the ethos of Peer Coaching is the support system it provides for adult workers. This in turn enhances the personal and professional respect among teachers. The coaching situation increases trust and energy level among teachers because through coaching they learn to share professional knowledge and skills. Too often teachers get training from people long removed from the classroom or from people who have never been in a classroom. Peer Coaching provides feedback from respected peers.

The role of the principal in Peer Coaching is to recognize the value of this collegial and structured sharing in renewing and restructuring schools. After a principal has been in a school three years, 85 percent of what does or does not happen is a direct result of his or her leadership. Therefore, principal leadership is one of the essential ingredients in Peer Coaching. The principal must be committed to the concept because she controls so many factors like the release time necessary for Peer Coaching. The principal must be willing to establish new norms, because with Peer Coaching teachers will no longer be able to go to their little rooms and close the doors. In successful schools, colleagues will share skills, practice, and knowledge with each other for the good of the student. The doors will be open to Peer Coaching. The "caves" will have walls with open windows and welcoming doors. The parking lot will no longer be the school's only common ground. Discussions in the lounge will focus on instruction instead of being the NBC Club: the nag, bitch, and complain club. Many reformers believe that each school now has within it the talent and resources to become a school of quality. Peer Coaching is a method to rely on that internal talent.

The visionary leader will also provide the planned participation by the whole faculty necessary for Peer Coaching to begin. Without planned participation at the beginning, there is almost no possibility that Peer Coaching will thrive. Teachers have too many other things to do to embrace another staff development program without strong principal support. The principal must have planned participation and the necessary release time to observe and coach. The principal who works smarter not harder will find ways to eliminate some nonessential duties of teachers so that they will not see Peer Coaching as an add-on. One way is to eliminate the next three faculty meetings. This may involve providing mutual planning times, finding coverage for a class, the principal covering a class, or replacing an inservice day with release time to balance that spent on Peer Coaching. The principal must also be prepared to provide the staff development that results from Peer Coaching requests from teachers. Once professionals engage in mutual problem solving, they begin to demand additional staff development training.

Role of the Principal or Administrator

The principal must:

1. be committed to the concept of Peer Coaching.
2. establish new norms. The teachers are accustomed to being alone in their classrooms. The principal must sell the faculty on the benefits of visiting and observing in classrooms for the improvement of instruction.
3. provide structure during the early stages of Peer Coaching, at least for the first two months.
4. identify exactly what support he will give to teachers who use Peer Coaching.
5. provide time in the schedule and coverage so that Peer Coaching can occur.
6. generate outside support for Peer Coaching.
7. provide staff development for Peer Coaching and other training areas that may result from concerns in Peer Coaching.
8. validate the use of Peer Coaching in teaching portfolios.

This model offers administrators a way to get more people involved in the improvement of instruction. By using the talent and resources present in local schools, the administrators can increase the number of persons involved in the improvement of instruction without an increase in budget. Peer Coaching helps professionalize teaching because it offers teachers a chance to be involved in decisions that impact them and their students.

IN THE CLASSROOM

A Scenario

As the students groan, Kaitlin, a second-grade teacher, is beginning a new unit in math to teach place value. Math has not been either the teacher's or the students' favorite subject, and the test scores have reflected that negative attitude. Kaitlin, however, has been to a staff development seminar to learn the old Korean finger-counting system, Chisanbop, and wants to use it to revitalize her teaching and to jump-start her students' learning and love of math. She thinks that Chisanbop will help students understand numeration and the whole process of math concepts and operations.

She begins the lesson by asking the students to put away their math workbooks, their pencils, and their papers. A clear desk is all they need to start. At this point, another teacher from the fifth-grade wing walks into the classroom, with pen and notepad, and sits quietly to the side of the room. The students are curious about her at first, but since she is only another teacher whom they see everyday, they soon become immersed in the lesson.

After about ten minutes, La Toya, the fifth-grade teacher, leaves quietly to pick up her own students from the art room. Immediately after the students leave for the day, La Toya drops by Kaitlin's classroom to talk about her visit and observations during the day. The teachers, who are peers (on the same level) converse briefly and pointedly about the factors Kaitlin had asked La Toya to observe. Kaitlin wanted to know what kind of feedback she gave her students as she introduced the Chisanbop unit. La Toya reads back the students' names from her seating chart and the comments or feedback Kaitlin gave to each as they began the math lesson. No feelings or judgments enter into the discussion. Kaitlin and La Toya discuss briefly the types of comments and the uniformity of Kaitlin's response of "Good!" Kaitlin asks La Toya to return in four days and record feedback again to see if more concentration on Kaitlin's part produces variation in student feedback.

The teacher has gotten the feedback she requested, and the coach has learned a few things to vary her own teaching strategies in fifth grade. Both agree that this process of peers coaching each other benefits the teacher, the coach, and most of all the student.

I have seen the above scenario repeated with great success in training and in actual practice with teachers in various schools. The five simple steps are:

1. The Teacher Requests a Visit
2. The Visit

3. The Coach Reviews the Notes and Lists Some Possibilities
4. The Talk after the Visit
5. The Review of the Process

The five steps and the rules have been followed without deviation into personal feelings or judgments on the part of the coach. By refraining from praising, the coach has helped the teacher look at the facts. By refraining from blaming, the coach has also helped the teacher look at the facts.

AT THE NATIONAL LEVEL

In 1990, John Goodlad published his landmark book, *Teachers for Our Nation's Schools,* after five years of research about what was wrong with teacher education. In 1991, he issued a call for colleges and universities to implement his nineteen preconditions for effective teacher perpetuation. From the hundreds who applied, Dr. Goodlad and his associates chose eight sites to begin the reform work. I became the state site director for the South Carolina site, which included a collaborative of five colleges: Benedict, Columbia, Furman, University of South Carolina, and Winthrop.

By 1998, the number of sites engaged with the Goodlad Initiative had increased to sixteen in fourteen states with 25 colleges, their teacher education and arts and sciences divisions, and about 400 professional development schools. The idea is to make equal partners of a local college (the education department and the arts and sciences departments) and local schools interested in becoming Professional Development Schools. These three equal partners reform and change teacher preparation.

At the state level, it was gratifying to me as a Peer Coaching designer to participate in a staff development training in July 1996 where public school teachers, college professors of education, and arts and sciences professors coached each other as they learned the Excel Corporation's 4 MAT Learning Styles.

At the national level, an example comes from the August 1997 annual conference of Goodlad's National Network for Educational Renewal. The week in Bellevue, Washington, brought together educators of all levels who had been engaged in educational renewal since the initial call in 1990. Each of the sixteen national sites made a presentation to highlight and summarize its work with arts and sciences departments and with Professional Development Schools. A wide variety of progress was noticeable. From the total involvement of the Hispanic schools and community surrounding the University of Texas at El Paso to the emerging collaborative of ten colleges in Nebraska, we could see educational renewal at work.

Even at this high-powered conference of educators who had been actively engaged in educational renewal for at least seven years, we saw a coaching requirement. As each of the sixteen sites planned its hour-long presentations and sent its title to Goodlad's Institute for Educational Inquiry, it was required to name and secure an educator from another site as its "coach" or "critical friend."

As state site director for the South Carolina collaborative of five colleges, I was able to select a coach or critical friend from one of the fifteen sites likewise engaged in educational renewal. It was important that the coach be a peer: not a dean from a small college or a large university which acted solo as a site in its state. We needed a real peer: one who worked with a collaborative of many colleges and/or one who knew about the diversity inherent in South Carolina's colleges. Our five colleges—Benedict, Columbia, Furman, USC, and Winthrop—represented a historically black college, a single-gender college, a private church-related college, the state's flagship research university and a former teacher training college. We had Brigham Young University and the University of Washington in our national network, but large research universities alone were not our site-peers.

Our coaching critical friends were our peers: Dr. Carol Wilson, who headed the five-college consortium in Colorado, and Dr. Nancy Gammon, a partner in the two-college consortium in St. Louis, Missouri. Dr. Gammon is also teacher education chair at Harris-Stowe College, which is a historically black college in St. Louis. Both coaches conversed with us by telephone and electronic mail as we planned our August 1997 presentation from South Carolina. Each coach had a specific problem to look for (à la Peer Coaching's Step 1: a Request from the teacher): Dr. Wilson watched for evidence of real collaboration among the five colleges and Dr. Gammon critiqued the synergy and interactive part of the presentation.

As the South Carolina presentation concluded, we "visited" with our peer coaches. We learned that not much evidence of collaboration was present and that the interactive part was limited, as the lecture mode dominated among teacher-educators. Our work was cut out for us as we worked to improve our performance for the gala "In Praise of Education" celebration planned for June 1999. Each of the sixteen sites had the charge to present its educational renewal work to the national audience. With the help of peer coaches from similar sites, the South Carolina Collaborative's presentation improved greatly from the August 1997 presentation.

As a worker for seven years in educational renewal, I was asked to coach the Missouri consortium's presentation and the ten-college Nebraska collaborative presentation. Each of the other sites had also chosen and worked with a peer who coached its August 1997 presentation so that the presentations would be excellent for June 1999. For the months between the two dates, coaches would communicate by e-mail or phone or visit their peer sites to work to improve presentations.

The most useful application of Peer Coaching is still teacher-to-teacher in schools' classrooms, but it is interesting to see deans, professors, directors, vice presidents, and teachers coach each other at national conferences of educational reformers such as Dr. Goodlad. If peer coaching can improve South Carolina's presentation at the June 1999 "In Praise of Education" gala, then it can assist classroom teachers also. Just think what errors the South Carolina group would have waded through unknowingly had they not requested coaching from their Colorado and Missouri peers!

CHAPTER 4

The Teacher Requests a Visit for Peer Coaching

Peer Coaching is a process, not content. It can only be used as the final step for any content staff development. After teachers have learned the new program, Peer Coaching is the final step that raises any newly learned staff development content to the 90 percent application level. It is only the completion of this step that will allow teachers to transfer any training to the classroom. But Peer Coaching can also be used to provide constant improvement to existing practices and to maintain any staff development training.

Beyond formal staff development programs, Peer Coaching can be used to improve practice. For example, a teacher wants to try a new technique on his own, so he approaches a fellow teacher also trained in Peer Coaching and says, "Barbara, I want to try cooperative learning in my social studies class. Will you help me plan and then coach me?" This is the optimum use of Peer Coaching—when it becomes internalized by teachers for everyday use. This increases teacher professionalism because, like other professions, the teachers learn to trust and respect their own professional judgment and that of their professional peers.

Shared decision making in how the school will use Peer Coaching is part of change and restructuring. Once the commitment is made to use Peer Coaching, then it is vital to decide *how* to use it. Otherwise it will be put on the shelf when next year's bandwagon comes along. Peer Coaching should be like an old pair of socks: simple and comfortable enough for everyday use. Like most new ventures, this first step is the most difficult. All the role players—principal, teacher, trainer—should aim toward this end: that Peer Coaching will be a vital and everyday part of the school's operation. Discussions of collegiality will become reality as teachers use coaching.

During the first phase, Peer Watching, the teachers do not actually request a Visit. All they have to do is to determine the time of the Visit. I suggest that every teacher initially be observed on the same skill, such as the opening focus or closure. This can be decided by the principal or by group decision making. This way, everyone in the school can be observed on the same skill.

Being observed on the same skill serves several purposes. This practice will also result in teachers discussing instruction. They will feel more confident and secure with the rules of Peer Coaching. If even this practice of Peer Watching seems threatening or radical, teachers could get used to having an observer in the classroom by videotaping themselves four or five times before instituting Peer Watching. Setting up a video camera or having a student assistant start the camera is a safe beginning for many isolated or overevaluated teachers. The teacher can then watch the video tape in the privacy of his own home and erase it. This allows the teacher time to look at his own techniques before exposing himself to a fellow teacher.

For instance, during the month of October, the team of teachers might decide that all teachers will practice Peer Watching with (1) wait-time or (2) questioning technique. During November, the team might decide that all will practice observing homework directions. Not only will this Peer Watching open the classroom doors, but it will also get isolated teachers used to watching and being watched by peers in a nonsupervisory, nonevaluative role. This comfort zone of Peer Watching will increase the possibility that real Peer Coaching will succeed. The hard part is to refrain from comments, evaluative or otherwise, during the Peer Watching phase.

The second phase of institutionalizing this model is Peer Feedback. In this phase, feedback or reflective listening is used without the real suggestions for improvement that come in true Peer Coaching. It is during this phase the pairs of teachers begin requesting a visit. Peer Feedback and Peer Coaching have the same first step: The Teacher Requests a Visit.

In clinical supervision, this first step is called the pre-conference. In Peer Coaching, the first step is called "The Teacher Requests a Visit." This title is deliberate to put the initiative in the hands of the professional teacher. We never request evaluation, but we as professionals can request coaching because we want to improve classroom practice for the benefit of students. The teacher must request a Visit because this increases professionalism by always putting it in the hands of the teacher. It also eliminates the fear associated with both evaluation and clinical supervision. This title also increases the chances that coaching will be used, because there is no connotation of either supervision or evaluation. It is just two or more peers helping each other.

The teacher may request a Visit for coaching on a new practice, maintaining a practice, a new idea, or just daily improvement. A great obstacle to overcome is this fear of asking someone for help being taken as a sign of weakness or an admission of incompetence. That fear has always been associated with evaluation or supervision. However, there is no stigma attached to one lawyer asking another how to play the jury. One football coach readily asks another how to defend against a single back set without fear of being labeled incompetent or weak. Who would want a doctor who would not consult with a colleague on proper dosage for a new medicine? Therefore, teachers must get to the place other professionals have been for years. It is not admitting weakness to ask for help. The only weakness is not asking a fellow professional. Teachers who are in the classroom daily usually have more knowledge about what works than a principal or training personnel who are no longer in the classroom every day.

In training for this step, participants should pair off and practice at least twice with real dialogue. Back in the classroom, it takes at least fifteen to twenty Visits before teachers internalize the everyday practice. At first the List of Possibilities (see chart 2) should be used for practice, until a teacher feels comfortable using his or her own concern for coaching. Practicing on a set list provides a safety net for using the steps before exposing oneself or taking a risk in front of a fellow teacher. Learning Peer Coaching, like any new and rewarding practice, won't be pretty or smooth at first. Performance and confidence may actually fall when peers observe and coach; but as confidence in the system grows, performance will improve.

If the feedback and coaching steps are to be successful, certain elements should be included in the Request for a Visit. Although it takes five minutes or less, the Request for a Visit should be done at least a day in advance of the actual visit so that coverage can be arranged for the coach.

The *teacher* chooses a peer coach and requests a Visit. The teacher's responsibility is to be very specific about what she wants the peer to observe. Most teachers will say, "Come and watch the discipline." At first, the request will be general in nature because teachers are not confident enough to be specific nor have been asked to define the observation. That is what evaluation has taught teachers: that someone else will define the area. Teachers will become more expert at dissecting teaching as they become more secure in professional Peer Coaching. All they need is the opportunity and encouragement to practice being peer coaches.

Chart 2. Some Possibilities for Peer Coaching Requests

Teacher questions, student responses, teacher follow-up
Handedness—teaching to right or left side, ignoring rest
Proximity—teacher movements indicated by arrows on seating chart
Wait-time
Male-female pattern of responses
Ethnicity patterns of responses
Learner responses: teacher in Talk after Visit indicates which students are high or low
Positive/negative statements by recording all statements
Praise/praise of learning
Kinds of reinforcement of correct and incorrect responses
All questions—teacher in Talk after Visit identifies levels of Bloom's taxonomy
Interaction with one student or one group
Time spent on materials, directions, or noninstructional talk
Material management and traffic flow
Student movement
List of teacher's non-content statements
Teacher's disciplinary comments
Opening set or focus
Closure or summary statement
Statement of objective
Question first or name first?
Clear explanation: list all steps or points
Student-to-student responses
Final ten minutes: student summary, teacher summary, sharing
Homework directions
Teacher talk time vs. student learning or guided practice time

The coach's job is to make sure she knows exactly what to observe. This requires the coach asking questions of the teacher or paraphrasing the Request. It may require probing to press the teacher to define a narrow range that can be observed in ten or fifteen minutes. The time limit is necessary until teachers get used to the Peer Coaching process. Never should a coach agree to visit unless she knows exactly what feedback the teacher is asking for and unless she feels that she can gather the data in the limited time available during the Peer Feedback phase.

There is an added advantage for this precise dissecting of the Request and the coach's probing questions for a narrowing of the specific concern. This practice forces two teachers to discuss and define for themselves elements of instruction that colleagues have never taken the opportunities to define. Usually the talk in the teachers' lounge centers around other items besides dissecting instruction. Probing and defining a specific Request begins the process of professionals discussing their profession: teaching.

Chart 3. Checklist for the Five Components

1. REQUEST FOR A VISIT (5 minutes)
    _____ observation request
    _____ specific concern defined
    _____ coach narrows concern
    _____ confidentiality established
    _____ no judgment or evaluation
    _____ lesson to be observed
    _____ data gathering method, both decide
    _____ seating chart, if necessary
    _____ observer-coach seating or placement
    _____ time/place
    _____ time for the Talk after Visit

Notes:
_____
_____
_____

2. THE VISIT (10 minutes)
    _____ request written at top of page as reminder
    _____ starting/ending time
    _____ method to be used to collect data
    _____ no judgment or evaluation

Notes:
_____
_____
_____

3. COACH REVIEWS NOTES AND
   LISTS SOME POSSIBILITIES OR SUGGESTIONS
    _____ coach reviewed data, deleted evaluation
    _____ teacher reviewed lesson performance and student activity
    _____ three leading questions listed on Coaching Form #1
    _____ no judgment or evaluation
    _____ suggestions listed on Coaching Form #2

Notes:
_____
_____
_____

4. TALK AFTER THE VISIT (5–10 minutes)
    _____ plan where to sit in relation to teacher
    _____ teacher or coach restatement of request in order to begin
    _____ stay away from "I" messages

Chart 3. (continued).

_____ coach goes over specific data collected and makes no outside observations
_____ careful not to be trapped by teacher's comments such as "What did you think of my lesson?"
_____ asks 3 leading questions to analyze data collected on the specific concern
_____ teacher analysis: get teacher talking
_____ no judgment or evaluation
_____ teacher request for coaching suggestions or alternatives
_____ teacher request for further observation
_____ coach gives teacher all notes or tapes
_____ schedule another session or exchange

Notes:

_____
_____
_____

5. PROCESS REVIEW: DID IT WORK FOR US? (3 minutes)
_____ teacher reaction to observation/coaching
_____ coach reaction to observation/coaching
_____ value of chosen data collection method
_____ conference strengths and weaknesses
_____ who learned the most?

Notes:

_____
_____
_____

Chart 4. Coaching Form #1

Request for Visit:

_____
_____
_____

Leading Questions:
1. _____
_____
2. _____
_____
3. _____
_____

Chart 5. Coaching Form #2

Suggestions for changes or improvements *when* the teacher requests them:

1. _____
   _____

2. _____
   _____

3. _____
   _____

The teacher and coach should assure each other that the confidentiality of the Peer Coaching process will not be violated. No aspect of Peer Coaching will ever be discussed in the lounge or anywhere else. Privacy and confidentiality are essential if trust is to become a reality.

The hardest part of Peer Coaching is to refrain from evaluation or judgment in the early stages. Teacher and coach should remind each other during step one that judgment and evaluation are not part of this process. This is a feedback session, which is an exchange between professionals concerning the gathering of data and does not require judgment. As trust and practice become firmly established, this assurance of no evaluation or judgment may become unnecessary.

The logistical arrangements in the Request should not be left to chance. Knowing the subject helps orient the observer, but it is not vital to Peer Coaching. The teacher should offer, or the coach should ask, what the lesson or new technique will be during the Visit, even if the Visit is for watching materials or discipline or proximity. The time and the place should be set and agreeable to the teacher and the coach. The principal can cover a class or arrange for coverage if no planning time is available. If necessary, the coach should ask for a seating chart. This is usually necessary only for Requests such as proximity, calling on students by name, or wait-time.

The coach needs to know where to sit when he or she comes into the room. Usually the back of the room is best, except when the coach needs to see student reactions. The seat should be placed in advance so that no disruption occurs. No greetings should be exchanged with the teacher or students by the coach. As use of Peer Coaching increases, the class will become accustomed to another teacher just entering and leaving with no comment. They will cease to react to other professionals being in the classroom.

During this step one, the Request for the Visit, the time should be set for the Talk after the Visit. It is essential that it take place as soon as possible. Immediately after the students leave for the day is best. Privacy must be assured and freedom from interruptions is essential so that the teacher feels secure from the beginning. Since people feel most secure in their own environment, it should take place in the teacher's classroom instead of the coach's classroom. A time limit should be set because the pair needs ample time to talk about the one concern, but not too much time so that it turns into a social gathering. Limiting the time for both the Visit and the Talk after the Visit will encourage more people to participate because they won't be worried about this excessive time.

In our practice, the Request takes five minutes and the Visit usually takes no more than ten to thirty minutes. The coach's review of the notes should take no more than five minutes in private. If the Talk after the Visit goes beyond five or ten minutes, socializing and the temptation to evaluate creep in. The Process Review takes a maximum of two minutes. The total process of this Peer Coaching takes no more than thirty minutes during a workday. Since the time is so limited, any professional can do it.

During the Request for the Visit, the teacher and the coach should mutually decide on what data gathering method will fit the observation. It needs to be as simple as possible to give the needed feedback, but it should not be intimidating to the coach or teacher. Self-designed forms or charts or tallies are best at first for the comfort zone. Stay away from detailed charts or forms designed by other people. Total script tape and verbatim notes are not a good idea at first because we are starting with only ten minutes and one focus or concern. As the comfort zone increases and trust grows, coach and teacher may resort to video tape or more detailed script tapes of the lesson observed.

SAMPLE DIALOGUE

The setting is after school on a hot September afternoon. Buddy comes into Barbara's social studies classroom and requests a Visit. They have both been trained in Peer Coaching.

Buddy the Teacher: "Barbara, would you be willing to come into my fifth-period class tomorrow and watch me as I try to improve sex equity?"

Barbara the Coach: "What do you mean by sex equity?"

Teacher: "I just read an article by the Sadkers that teachers spend eight times more time instructing males than females. Females don't score as high on science as males do. Maybe this is the reason. Will you come to my class and see how I do?"

Coach: "I'm still not sure what you want me to do. Do you want me to see how much females participate? How can I take notes on that? What exactly can I record?"

Teacher: "Tally how many females I call on."

Coach: "What would that tell you? Would it give you a comparison?"

Teacher: "No, I guess not. What else could we use instead of a tally?"

Coach: "I could tally every time you ask a male a question and every time you ask a female a question. That would give some comparison, but what else could we do?"

Teacher: "Could you record the questions that I ask as well as whether males or females are called on? Maybe that could show the level of questions I am asking males and what level of questions I am asking females."

Coach: "Okay, I can do that, but I will just write down the question so that later we can both decide what level of Bloom's taxonomy each question is on. I will write down beside each question whether you asked a male or female student to answer. Would it help if I jotted the time down in the margin?"

Teacher: "I'm afraid that would be too much for this Visit. Let's just stay with who I call on and what the question is."

Coach: "Okay. You must know I have a planning period fifth period tomorrow or you wouldn't have asked me."

Teacher: "Well, I do admit I checked the schedule, but you are one I could trust not to talk about this coaching in the teachers' lounge."

Coach: "I won't, you know. Do you want me to come in the beginning, middle, or end of the period? How long do you want me to stay?"

Teacher: "Come in five minutes after the period starts. The question segment of this lesson will last approximately fifteen minutes. I'll have a chair placed in the back of the room just as you come in the door."

Coach: "Well, great, but I can really only stay ten minutes. I need to leave to grade my tests during my planning period, so I will get up and leave after ten minutes."

Teacher: "Okay, I appreciate your coming for ten minutes and I will expect you to leave whether or not I'm finished with the questions. I think that will give me a good sample of my questioning of students."

Coach: "Do I need a seating chart?"

Teacher: "I don't think so. I'm more concerned with whether it's a male or female I call on, not where they are sitting or their names.

Coach: "What lesson are you teaching?"

Teacher: "Checks and balances in American government. Is there anything else you need?"

Coach: "If I come in early and you are not ready to question, just cue me when you want me to start recording. You know I'm not coming to judge or evaluate, just to provide some feedback and some suggestions that might help with your concern."

Teacher: "Yeah, I understand. I've learned my lesson and I won't ask you how well I did. When could we talk about the visit? When will you have time to review your notes?"

Coach: "It will push me, but I think I can be ready right after school. How about twenty minutes after the students leave today? In your classroom?"

Teacher: "Okay. Thanks, I'll be interested in what your notes show me."

CHAPTER 5

The Visit

This part of Peer Coaching is called a Visit so that it is collegial and user-friendly. It can be compared to a business person visiting another person's place of business frequently and informally. The whole point of Peer Coaching is to make this happen frequently and informally in the classroom to end teacher isolation and to increase professionalism. It is also called a Visit so that the teacher and the students will find it a natural occurrence to have other people in the classroom.

Once when I was teaching second grade and using Peer Coaching with the Success Reading and Writing program, the second-graders and I had become so accustomed to having people in the classroom, I looked up and saw twenty-three extra people in the classroom. They were not disturbing the students or me because Visits had become such a part of the daily routine.

The Visit should be both enjoyable and beneficial for both the teacher and coach. It should in no way be intrusive for the teacher nor threatening on the part of the coach. Instead, the Visit should be an opportunity for professional growth for both teacher and coach. Many teachers have told us that they have learned as much or more acting as coach as they have being coached. Not only is the coach picking up extra things outside the focus by osmosis, he is also honing his instructional skills by dissecting the observed teaching concern. These visits tell the students that instruction is being emphasized because they will see teachers who will use whatever means are at their disposal to improve skills so that students can learn more.

Strict parameters should be observed to make the first Visits successful. The teacher and coach each have responsibilities. The coach walks in and finds the assigned seat. The coach should be as invisible as possible while entering or exiting. She should not speak to students, give them high fives, wave to comrades, slap them on the back, or otherwise interact. She should have the data gathering form prepared by coach and teacher ready with pen in hand. No comments should be offered by the coach either aside or on the lesson. Her demeanor should indicate that she is there on business. If students persist, a firm but tough smile should indicate that the coach is here to observe.

Beginning time should be recorded at the top of the page. If the teacher is not yet at the point of the requested concern, the coach watches carefully for the prearranged signal that indicates the starting point. During the information gathering phase, the coach must focus her entire attention to the requested concern. She must gather data on only the information requested by the teacher. If other things that happen that are interesting, the coach should ignore them. The coach must remember that even intervention in discipline matters is forbidden. The coach is not there to judge classroom procedures, but to gather information on the teacher's request. Focus on the one request builds trust and confidence. The coach should remember that all classrooms are different and there is more than one way to skin a cat. This perspective should help the coach focus on the single objective, which is to gather information on the teacher's request.

What if the teacher never gets to the part he asked the coach to observe? If some discipline problem intervenes or if the teacher simply goes in a different direction than planned, then the coach should quietly leave when the allotted time is reached. She should never try to guess or record something that was not requested. This also ensures professional respect and can be discussed in the Talk after the Visit.

Another problem that may occur is that the agreed upon data gathering method may not work in the actual classroom. If the method the coach is prepared to use does not match the request, he may just drop it and observe. Later the teacher and coach can work out another device and arrange another visit. Remember that this is not evaluation or supervision: two peers can work it out together. Another option is to quickly adapt that device or use a simple alternative. Again the failure of the data gathering device should be discussed in the Talk after the Visit. The teacher always has the option of saying whether the desired information was useful and if another device should be used.

Once the allotted time is up, the coach should leave. The coach should feel no obligation to stay beyond the time limit even if the teacher is not finished. If the coach stays longer, it is a hardship on the person covering her class. It also encourages the teacher in meandering around the point. These misgivings can be detrimental to the entire Peer Coaching process. A little thing like being five minutes late back to class may make it hard to get voluntary coverage the next time. It is paramount that the coach keep up with the time, enter at the agreed time, and leave at the agreed time limit. The teacher should not expect more or less than the agreed-upon time.

The initial rules and time limits are very important in the beginning to keep both teacher and coach focused on the time. Much can be gained through the coaching process if it is kept short and used frequently. Another advantage that Peer Coaching has over supervision is that the observation is much more flexible. It can last from ten to fifty minutes, whereas evaluative observations usually last an hour. They also take an hour to prepare and debrief. The usual observation makes the teacher prepare a showcase lesson to fit the time. With Peer Coaching, the teacher may request a Visit on one focus that may happen in any lesson. The daily routine or normal progression is upset by a traditional observation. In Peer Coaching, the coaching fits into the normal lesson with just one concern dissected. Teacher and coach feel more comfortable dealing with one focus at a time instead of the whole lesson.

A SAMPLE VISIT: NO DIALOGUE

On Thursday before fifth period, Buddy makes sure the chair for Coach Barbara is in the designated spot. Buddy has told the students that a visitor is coming and that no special attention is necessary.

Fifth period begins at 1:05, and at 1:10 Barbara walks quietly into the room and sits down without talking to the students or the teacher. She has her notepad and her pen ready. Buddy's request is written at the top of her notepad to remind her what the focus is. She notes the starting time and the agreed-upon time limit of ten minutes.

The teacher is teaching the lesson and does not acknowledge the visitor. He is aware that the coach is here to observe the questioning phase and moves quickly into that part of the lesson.

The coach records each question as it is asked and whether it was directed to a male or a female. But several times, as the teacher calls on a female, a male intervenes. This presents a problem since there was no discussion about how to gather these data. The coach makes a note of this information in case the teacher wants these data later. She notes male, volunteer, or puts a star beside the female's name and notes that a male intervened without being called upon by the teacher.

At the end of the ten minutes, the coach gets up and leaves without fanfare. The teacher continues with the lesson.

Many teachers miss the point of the Request for a Visit because they think that by voicing the concern and having an observer that the skill is automatically showcased. In my experience, this never happens because the teacher reverts to the natural state with an unobtrusive observer. The coach then gets a true picture of actual practice because it is part of the daily routine. Sometimes planning and having a Visit results in better instruction on the part of the teacher. If this happens, the desired outcome — improvement of instruction — is still accomplished.

The Visit seems to be the most simple step in Peer Coaching, but following the defined parameters in this step leads to success. Like all the other steps, the Visit is under the control of the teacher and has as its focus the improvement of instruction.

CHAPTER 6

The Coach Reviews the Notes and Lists Some Possibilities

Although my experience has shown that this part usually takes only five to ten minutes, this preparation in review and writing is crucial to the success of the whole process. What the coach does in this step lays the ground-work for a successful Talk after the Visit. Time spent reviewing the notes and the data collection here will pay off double when the conference is held. Good conferences do not happen automatically. Being a good teacher does not mean that a person is automatically a good coach. It takes preparation and careful forethought. The checklist featured in chart 3 is a useful tool for organizing this process.

This preparation should take place in a quiet and private place so that ten minutes of reflection is profitable. It is essential to this reflective model of Peer Coaching that the coach focus entirely on reviewing the data.

It takes a tactful approach to walk the tightrope between feelings and the improvement of instruction. The coach must not assume that the teacher can take feedback impersonally just because he asked for a Visit. The coach must still be tactful and thoughtful. This is especially true when it is very apparent the data show great cause for concern on the teacher's Request. The coach must keep in mind that above all the continuing collegial relationships are more important than the success of any one Visit. Without relationships of trust and confidence, there will be no more Visits.

While reviewing the notes, the coach must be careful to remove any evaluative comments—even those such as "Great!" and smiley faces. The notes become the property of the teacher. The first hint of any evaluation or judgment will do irreparable damage to the process of Peer Coaching. The coach should compute any necessary numbers beforehand, such as tallying the number of times girls or boys were called on. Note the times and add the minutes if it is important. All of this should be in an easy-to-read format so the coach can walk the teacher through the data, and so that the teacher can see at a glance what went on during the Visit.

Now for the writing part. The coach must write down three things:

1. The opening statement for the Talk after the Visit
2. Two to four leading questions to get the teacher to reflect on the lesson.
3. Two to four suggestions for improvement if the teacher is receptive (asks for them).

It is always important to focus on the original Request. A good opening statement is something like "Remember you asked me to collect data on . . . calling on males and females and writing down the question?" The reason we do this is to avoid things like the teacher asking, "Well, how did I do?" or the coach saying, "How do you *feel* about the lesson?" It brings the focus entirely on the Request for the Visit, not personality or the per-formance of the teacher or the performance of the students in the class. Focus on the Request prevents endless discussion about students, their behavior, classroom incidents, or feelings.

Chart 6. Peer Coaching: Dos and Don'ts

DO
1. Listen actively.
2. Pause . . . and make reflective statements.
3. Insert neutral probing questions to get the peer to continue reflection.
4. Bite your tongue . . . and let the teacher talk.
5. Let the teacher fill the gaps of silence, not you.
6. Review only the written data.
7. Leave other concerns for other visits.
8. Refer to the safety of the Peer Coaching rules.
9. Offer to gather data using a different method.
10. Lead into another Visit or exchange.

DON'T
1. Praise.
2. Blame.
3. Judge.
4. Set yourself as an example.
5. Offer solutions on your own not supported by research or practice.
6. Repeat the content of the coaching session to other colleagues.
7. Offer data that is not written as observed.
8. Examine concerns that were not requested: offer no sidelines.
9. Offer to break the Peer Coaching rules.
10. Praise or blame—worth repeating.

The coach must avoid starting the conference with any opening statement that would lead to a discussion of *feelings* instead of facts. It is just like research: we must use the factual basis first if any improvement or change is to happen.

After writing the opening statement (on Coaching Form #1 in chart 4), which repeats the Request ("Remember you asked me to collect data on . . ."), the coach must write the hardest part. The two to four leading questions to get the teacher to reflect on the lesson are difficult to write. They require much thought and tact from the coach. The questions should be neutral to get the teacher to talk. We usually think that the teacher will have no trouble talking about the lesson, but teachers are accustomed to supervisors leading the discussion or analyzing the lesson. That is why it is important to structure leading questions so that the teacher will take the time to reflect and dissect the lesson. This means that the questions should be phrased so that the teacher does most of the talking.

A neutral leading question that meets these guidelines is: "Here are the data I gathered. What does this tell you?" Another good question is: "Can you use these data to change instruction?" or "What decisions can you make now?"

The coach will not write any question that could possibly be answered yes or no. The point is to start the teacher talking. Ineffective questions include: "Why did you do what you did here?" "How do you *feel* the lesson went?" "You don't have anything to worry about because those kids misbehave in my class too." The point of taking time to write down leading questions is to provoke the teacher to talk and to engage in self-analysis of the lesson.

On a separate sheet of paper or Coaching Form #2 (from chart 5 or appendix 1), the coach now writes down two or three suggestions for improvement to use if the teacher is receptive. These suggestions should also be nonjudgmental and nonevaluative. The suggestions should convey a non-"I" message: not saying what I would do, but what might be helpful. *No suggestion should begin with I.* It is important to have two or three, because too many will turn the teacher off or put him on defensive. One conscientious coach listed ten to deliver. By the time he reached number five, the teacher was angry and defensive and asked, "Wasn't there anything you liked about the lesson?" If the coach has ten suggestions, she should still pick out the two or three most powerful and save the others for another time.

The teacher will be more receptive to statements that begin with "Some people have found that this works . . ." in place of "I do it this way. . . ."

The coach should try "You know I've run into this also. Maybe we could work out a solution together," instead of "I have the solution to your problem." The point here is that the coach works hard on writing down suggestions that avoid setting herself up as the superior or master teacher who is judging. If the teacher is not receptive to suggestions for improvement, this separate sheet of paper (Coaching Form #2) should be destroyed.

Thorough preparation for the Talk after the Visit will prove helpful for the coach as well as for the teacher. In our profession of teaching, one of the greatest barriers to improvement of instruction is not taking even a few minutes to reflect on practice. These skills have never been developed and refined because we have not taken the time to self-analyze or to dissect lessons. This is not a skill that we are taught as undergraduates or even as graduates and certainly not as novice teachers. If these skills are ever to be developed, they must be practiced in a supportive environment with trusted colleagues. It has been my experience that the coach often learns more than the teacher because she must develop the dissecting skills, the listening skills, and the observing skills.

CHAPTER 7

The Talk after the Visit

The critical attribute of Peer Coaching is the Talk after the Visit. If this step is successful, then Peer Coaching will continue to be used in the school for the improvement of instruction. This is where the work of the coach and the teacher pay off and where the seed is planted for any future sessions of Peer Coaching. The careful preparation which the coach did in reviewing her notes and listing possibilities pays off in this step.

By keeping to one focus, the coach and the teacher can dissect the requested concern in the lesson and keep away from the feelings and behaviors of teacher or students. The coach must continue to observe the teacher's reaction during the feedback and coaching so that the coach can observe the teacher's readiness to accept suggestions. The coach must observe verbal and nonverbal cues as the session progresses. He must practice active listening skills with frequent pauses. This technique, combined with the prepared leading questions, keeps the teacher talking and dissecting his own lesson.

As suggested earlier, the Talk after the Visit should take place in the teacher's classroom at a time when there will be no interruptions. The conference in the teacher's own territory gives the teacher a sense of confidence and control. The seating arrangements should be positioned so that teacher and coach are sitting side by side so that they can look at the notes together. A table with two chairs on the same side is ideal. Whenever a desk is used, the one seated behind the desk gives the impression of the superior position. Any other chair drawn up to the desk is a subordinate position. If more than two are in the session, chairs should be in a circle so that all can share equally. No one should be at the head of the table or appear to be in charge because of the position of the chairs.

All this positioning of chairs may seem like going into too much detail, but unequal seating denotes differences in status and damages all that teacher control and collegiality that has been carefully built. Attention

63

should be paid to all details to ensure that the teacher feels that he or she is in control of the conference and does most of the talking.

We must remember that long years of the teacher in the subordinate position in evaluation has built barriers. Desk barriers and superior chairs are power plays that have been taught to some supervisors. The inferior position has always given the teacher the feeling "I am not here to participate, I am here to be told!" Working hard at first to ensure equality in seating arrangements is very important to overcome years of deliberate barriers. At first, the teacher will not feel comfortable sitting side by side in what he perceives as a judging experience. It takes some time to get used to the sharing position. Attention to these small details is critical to the success of the Talk after the Visit. (See chart 3.)

Although in all of our training sessions, we stress seating and body language, when we break into pairs to practice, most pairs assume a superior-subordinate position. It is very difficult to overcome years of ingrained habit. Often when we as trainers correct this error, the two are not even aware that they have assumed these positions. Another error that most are not even aware of until we point it out is the perceived "superior" gesturing with a pencil to command attention.

This minor detail of the commanding pencil illustrates that body language is even more important than seating arrangement. Pencil waving is associated in the teacher's mind with the evaluator or the supervisor. In an evaluative situation, the supervisor controls the content of the conference by keeping the notes or data collection to herself instead of sharing the notes side by side with the teacher. The sharing position is always important between professional peers.

Closed or open body language is extremely important at the beginning and all during the conference. The coach should not send any closed signals such as arms crossed or face or body averted. Although the coach should be aware of the short and focused time, she should not constantly look at a watch or clock because it sends a powerful signal that the conference should be ending. Uncrossed arms or gestures indicate openness. Sitting erect indicates interest and intensity. Leaning back on a tilted chair with hands clasped behind the head indicates power instead of openness. Five minutes of open body language and active listening is not too much to ask of any professional educator in the role of teacher or coach. This is a learned skill and needs to be frequently practiced in this and other situations. Attention to these details will assist teacher and coach in other aspects of their responsibilities as instructional leaders. People interested in learning more about active listening should read Thomas Gordon's *Leadership Effectiveness Training* (1977).

Points from Gordon's active listening include:

1. Avoid ordering, directing, commanding.
2. Avoid warning, admonishing, moralizing, preaching.
3. Avoid advising, giving solutions or suggestions.
4. Avoid lecturing, teaching, giving logical examples.
5. Avoid judging, criticizing.
6. Avoid disagreeing, blaming.
7. Avoid praising, agreeing.
8. Avoid name-calling, ridiculing, shaming.
9. Avoid interpreting, analyzing, diagnosing.
10. Avoid reassuring, sympathizing, consoling, supporting.
11. Avoid probing, questioning, interrogating.
12. Avoid withdrawing, distracting, humoring, diverting.

These points about active listening are also reflected in Peer Coaching, especially points 6 and 7: no praise, no blame. The coach as an active listener helps the peer being coached work out solutions himself by acting as the reflective listener.

In an interview with Pauline Gough (1987), William Glasser talks about interviewing high school students, asking them if they felt important in this school. Glasser said that he might as well have asked, "Are you horseradish around here?" because the question of importance had no meaning for students. It was not even in their universe of possibilities to be important in school. But the same question can be asked of teachers: Are you important (or horseradish) around here? Power is important to people, thus the minor attention to details in this conference so that power is shared. Using Glasser's principles, later we talk about Peer Coaching becoming fun and part of the power structure in schools.

Time is crucial. Both the teacher and coach should agree upon five or ten minutes for the Talk after the Visit. In my experience, I have found in the early stages that the concern can be addressed in this short period. Once the concern is addressed, the Talk should end. There is always the temptation to comment on things other than the requested concern and that may cause the pair to lose or dilute the focus. As the requested concerns become more complex and we become more experienced in providing feedback and coaching, the time can be expanded. In no coaching situation should the pair try to improve all areas of the teaching act. The point of Peer Coaching under control of teachers is to use it frequently by keeping it as short as possible.

As the coach walks into the teacher's classroom and exchanges greetings, she finds the ideal seating arrangement. No extended pleasantries
should be exchanged nor other items discussed, because this tends to dilute the brief and focused point of having the conference. The Talk after
the Visit begins with the carefully planned opening statement. The coach
begins with "Remember you asked me to . . ." and she restates the
teacher's Request for the Visit. This sets a professional tone to dissect the
lesson. Two professionals will now begin analyzing the facts gathered and
come to conclusions about the concern.

There is a natural tendency for the coach to open with compliments or
to give "warm fuzzies." In my experience with Peer Coaching, compliments detract from the focus of this interaction. There is always another
time and place for the warm fuzzies. If the coach says, "I enjoyed the lesson" as an opening statement, the teacher waits only for the "but" that in-
evitably follows. This is difficult for the teacher because he is accustomed
to hearing the evaluator's positive opening statement. It is also difficult
for the coach because she is concerned about hurting the teacher's feelings
if no compliment is offered. Both the teacher and the coach must realize
that compliments are forms of evaluation and might divert the session into
an evaluative mode. This goes against the number one principle of Peer
Coaching, which is to be nonevaluative. When compliments or warm
fuzzies dilute the opening statement, the effectiveness of this Peer Coaching model is compromised. Frequency and brevity are the mottoes of this
nonjudgmental, nonevaluative model.

After the opening statement ("Remember you asked me to . . ."), the
coach walks through the data with the teacher, sharing the notes or data
collection between them. The notes have been summarized and high-
lighted so that they are easy for the teacher and the coach to analyze. If
the data are not arranged in an easy to read manner, it slows down the
process of analyzing the lesson. More energy should be spent on interpreting the data, not on trying to decipher them. The coach should begin
by asking her prepared leading questions as they finish looking at the data.
She might ask, "What does this information tell you?"

If this is the information the teacher wanted, he can begin to analyze
how to improve or change. It is the coach's job to continue with the prepared leading questions to probe and provoke the teacher to analyze further. The coach might ask another probing question, such as "What decisions can you make now?" The teacher must now reflect on his decision
about change or improvement in the area of the requested visit. Pronouns
used during this step should always be "you" and "we"—never "I." "I"

statements on the part of the coach tend to set her up as the authority or the master teacher and allow her to dominate the conversation.

This is a reflective coaching model and the purpose of the Talk after the Visit is to have the teacher reflect on the concern and do most of the talking. The major responsibility of the coach during this step is to keep the teacher talking. At times the teacher may ask for direct comment from the coach. This is okay, if the coach does not take it as an opportunity to dominate the session. If this is a group session, the teacher should still do most of the talking. Many models of Peer Coaching use this step to lead to evaluation, but that is not the purpose of this model. This model is focused on getting all teachers involved in self-analysis with the help of a peer so that coaching can happen frequently and under the control of the teachers.

Active listening and the leading questions become equally important during this step. After the coach asks a leading question, she must pause, use the skills of active listening, such as counting to ten. We must overcome the discomforting felling that silence brings. Reflection requires thinking time and counting to ten allows some thinking time. The hardest part of Peer Coaching is biting your tongue, especially when something seems obvious to the coach, but not to the teacher. Biting one's tongue or counting to ten develops active listening skills. True learning is enhanced when the teacher reaches the conclusion himself after looking at the data and reflecting. It is hard to break the dependence on the evaluator who has always told the teacher the conclusion.

Active listening skills such as silence and pausing allow the teacher time to think, but they also allow the coach reflective opportunities to formulate additional probing questions based on the teacher's reaction. The written planned questions may not be appropriate as the reflective process continues. Unless the coach is actively listening, she may not pick up clues and may continue with the planned questions. She should use the clues and silences to formulate more relevant reflective questions. Often the coach is so eager to get to the suggestions that she does not take advantage of the opportunities to improve the quality of the Talk after the Visit. At times, even though the coach is not using the pronoun "I," she is still thinking about what she is going to say next instead of listening to the teacher's reflections.

The old adage is very important here: Why do you have two ears and only one mouth? So you can listen twice as much as you talk.

A major problem that frequently occurs in training is nodding the head in agreement with what the teacher is saying. Traditionally the nod connotes approval. To some, it means, "I understand." The coach will find it difficult to refrain from nodding, but she should remember to act as if she were a video camera which has been rewound and set on Play. It is difficult to break years of habit with traditional evaluation and warm fuzzies, but this model has a different purpose. As an alternative to head nods, the coach should merely look at the teacher in a direct and open manner. If the coach thinks about the little dog dolls in cars, endlessly nodding their jointed heads, it may help the coach restrain her nodding. If the coach starts nodding and then stops, the teacher may take it as a negative. It is best to refrain from nodding so signals cannot be misinterpreted.

Another trap for the coach is questions the teacher may ask to solicit evaluative information from the coach. Despite the fact that both coach and teacher accept the rules and structure of Peer Coaching, many teachers will still try to elicit approval as we have always done with evaluators or supervisors. A question asked frequently in the infant stages of Peer Coaching implementation is "How did I do?" The coach has a canned reply, "Remember I am not here to evaluate, just to give you feedback on the Request for the Visit." If the coach constantly refuses to fall in the trap, it is no problem.

This is still the feedback part of Peer Coaching, reviewing the data and reflecting on the data. No suggestions for improvement are yet offered. Feedback statements should be:

- Specific in nature
- About items the teacher can control
- Solicited rather than imposed
- Descriptive rather than evaluative
- Tactful
- Well timed
- Checked for clarity and simplicity
- Dealing with behaviors rather than personalities (of either teacher or students)
- Data-driven not personality-driven
- Thoughtfully planned beforehand
- Well organized

Feedback should not be:

- Generalized
- On items outside the teacher's control
- Given on anything other than the request

- Feelings
- Directive
- Too long
- Difficult to interpret
- An "I" message
- Ambiguous
- Repetitious

TRUE COACHING

After the feedback is complete and the traps have been avoided, the coach should pause. Suggestions for improvement should only be offered if the teacher has thoroughly analyzed the data and is ready to hear the prepared suggestions. This is the stage that requires the utmost tact and diplomacy. Keep in mind that the total professional relationship is more important that this one session of Peer Coaching. The teacher should also keep in mind that any instruction can stand some improvement and that he should never hesitate to ask this peer coach for suggestions.

Although even outstanding teachers say that we are now ready to be coached, what we *really* want to hear is that the lesson was perfect. It is difficult to break the belief that asking for a suggestion is admitting weakness. Unlike other professionals, teachers rarely seek advice and even more rarely take it. One problem is that we say that we are professionals, but we do not treat our peer teachers as professionals. We treat others, such as supervisors, textbook authors, and outside consultants, as if they are the real teaching professionals. We treat these others as if they knew more about what should happen in the classroom than our peer teachers who are still there every day, in the trenches with us.

In my experience with implementing Peer Coaching in schools and colleges, I have found that those most willing to accept coaching are the master teachers. In one elementary school, every teacher was trained in Peer Coaching and the administration supported it with released time. Not much happened until an outstanding second-grade teacher was transferred to fifth grade. She came to a fellow teacher and asked to be observed teaching writing to fifth graders. She said that what she had used with great results with younger students did not work with older students. She pleaded with the coach to give suggestions for improving her teaching of writing. Once it was apparent that this master teacher asked a peer for help, others began asking for coaching also.

Sara Levine has discussed the phases and stages of growth and development of adult learners in her book *Promoting Adult Growth in Schools* (1989). Both she and Erik Erikson list separate and distinct characteristics of teachers or learners in progressive age groups. Participants in Peer Coaching may want to become more familiar with these characteristics to become more effective at coaching.

Roland Barth, in *Improving Schools from Within* (1990), describes three general kinds of teachers:

1. One type does not want to look at himself critically nor does he wish others to do so.
2. A second type will look at herself critically but does not want anyone else to do so.
3. The outstanding teacher is willing to look at himself critically and requests others to offer suggestions.

Barth discusses the importance of collegiality and bringing all teachers to the third category. The administrator who provides time, training, and support for this to happen is an instructional leader. The Peer Coaching process gives instructional leaders who are willing to invest the time and energy a way to move teachers to Barth's goal.

No matter which category the teacher is in, it is important during the Talk after the Visit to keep the suggestions to a maximum of three. Even the master teacher does not want to be overwhelmed. In my experience, more than three suggestions causes the teacher to feel defensive. More than three suggestions may also change the tone of the conference and create a negative atmosphere. Even though the coach has more than three suggestions, he should select only the most powerful and the ones that have a better chance of working. The coach should avoid suggesting watching another master teacher unless the teacher directly asks if the coach knows someone who performs this skill exceptionally well. In no instance should the coach offer himself as the master of this technique. However, the coach can say, "I have had this concern also. Could you observe me teaching it and then maybe we could work on a mutual solution that we could both use?"

The coach can also say, "I do not know the answer to this concern. Perhaps the pair of us or a group of us can find an expert to develop our skills in this one area." The answer might lie in further training, staff development, or a workshop by a college expert. There is no stigma attached to admitting "I don't know." As a matter of fact, it is better to admit this than to offer a tip or suggestion with no knowledge base.

Coaching suggestions are often more effective when posed in the form of a question to the teacher. In one training session, a teacher wanted to help students who were having difficulty with a dance step. She tried to demonstrate the step and observe the students trying it at the same time. When her back was turned during the demonstration, she missed the three students who were having difficulty. During the coaching session, the coach avoided saying, "You must face the students." Instead he said, "When can you stop the demonstration and observe all the students as the practice?" This coaching statement made the teacher decide when to pause in the demonstration and concentrate totally on observing difficulties in practice. "When" statements are much more useful to the teacher than "how" or "why" statements. He can make a decision about a point in time in the lesson to do it instead of defending why he does it. Helpful statement by the coach include:

- Some teachers have used. . . .
- You know, I've had the same concern. Maybe you could observe me and we could work out a mutual solution.
- Have you ever considered trying. . . .
- When can you use this in the lesson?
- Have you seen the research on this concern?

Never say:

- You should teach it this way.
- Why did you do what you did?
- I have the solution to your problem.
- Go observe Mr. Goodteacher. He does it correctly.
- You need a workshop or course in. . . .
- You have nothing to worry about. Those kids misbehave in my class also.

As the Talk after the Visit draws to a conclusion, the coach makes a point of giving the teacher all the notes and suggestions from the coaching session. She does not keep copies nor send copies to the principals nor allow other teachers to look at the notes. By giving the notes to the teacher, the coach reinforces the fact that the teacher is in control of this process. It also builds trust and confidentiality. If, for any reason, the teacher and coach did not reach the true coaching stage of suggestions for improvement, the suggestions page should be destroyed. This is why it is important to write the suggestions on a separate page from the notes or the leading questions. (See chart 5.)

A humorous way to end the session is for the coach to reassure the teacher that this will not be discussed in the lounge or anywhere else. This joking comment will reassure the teacher that this coaching will remain confidential and that it is a professional exchange between respected peers. The last question should be: "Who is holding the notes?"

A SAMPLE DIALOGUE FOR THE TALK AFTER THE VISIT

It is 3:15 P.M., with the students dismissed for the day and teachers remaining until 3:45 P.M. Coach Barbara walks into Teacher Buddy's class room.

Barbara the Coach: "Hi, Buddy. How's it going?"
Buddy the Teacher: "Hi, Barbara. It's been a rough day. I'm glad it's 3:15."
Coach: "Are you ready for the Talk after the Visit?"
Teacher: "Sure. Pull up one of those student desks."
Coach: "Why don't we sit here at your worktable together so that we both see the notes at the same time?"
Teacher: "Okay, how about a soft drink?"
Coach: "Sure. Let's see what we have here."
Teacher: "Well, how did you think the lesson went today?"
Coach: "Remember that Peer Coaching is not evaluation. I'm here to give you feedback. Just the facts, ma'am."
Teacher: "I forgot that is contrary to the rules of Peer Coaching. Let's look at what you got."
Coach: "Remember you asked me to tally the number of males and females you called on. You also asked me to write down the questions."
Teacher: "Right. I did."
Coach: "Look at these questions I wrote down from 1:10 until 1:20."
Teacher: "Looks like I called on seven males and two females during this ten-minute period."

Coach: "Does this tally tell you anything?"

Teacher: "It sure does! Even though you were there watching and I was concentrating on equity, I still reverted to my usual practice of calling on more males than females. I would have thought I would do better than that since I had asked you to observe this particularly. What does this asterisk mean?"

Coach: "Well, you actually called on two more females, but each time a male intervened and answered instead of the female you called on."

Teacher: "I guess the Sadkers' research was correct in this one lesson anyway. I've got to be more conscious of calling on females in my government class."

Coach: "Let's look at the types of questions you asked during these ten minutes."

Teacher: "I was aiming for all of them to be above the knowledge or recall level. Let's see how successful I was."

Coach: "Here are the nine questions you asked."

Teacher: "Well, it looks to me like they are all above the knowledge level. Except this one might be on the knowledge level. Do you agree?"

Coach: "Yes."

Teacher: "I think I did well on the questions, but not on equity. Do you have any ideas about how I can improve in this area?"

Coach: "Have you considered calling the name last?"

Teacher: "Is that really going to help me with the equity?"

Coach: "At least it's a reminder of which gender you are calling on each time. Have you considered writing down the questions and also the student's name?"

Teacher: "Great, I like that idea. I wrote down the questions so I could be sure to go above recall level. It would not be too much extra trouble to write down student names. The right question is very important to understanding this stuff."

Coach: "Did I collect the facts you wanted this time? Should I come back again?"

Teacher: "Let me work on this way of questioning and you come back next Thursday."

Coach: "After that, would you come in and observe me asking questions about maps? I'm wondering what I actually do with equity in questioning."

Teacher: "Okay. By the way, who gets these notes?"

Coach: "Thanks for reminding me. These are your property."

CHAPTER 8

The Process Review
and Reflection on Peer Coaching

This final step in Peer Coaching should take only two or three minutes. The sole purpose is to improve the process the teacher and coach have just experienced. Both people review the rules and guidelines to see how closely they were followed. It is also an opportunity to set the stage for the next Peer Coaching session with this pair or group. In some instances the pair may want to tape record their Talk after the Visit, so that it will be easier to review adherence to the guidelines or checklist.

The Process Review should take place in the teacher's classroom immediately after the Talk after the Visit. It can blend in very naturally with step four with no division except the recognition that the two are concluding by reviewing the process. A reflective model always forces the participants to pause and reflect on practice. This is an essential part of any learning process: requiring people to take time to think about what just happened. This step in the process requires both coach and teacher to step back from this particular lesson and focus solely on the process.

It is not necessary that the teacher do most of the talking in this step. The coach should assume the responsibility to see that this Process Review takes place. Although it is not important who talks the most in this step, certain questions must be asked and answered. These questions should be discussed:

- Who talked the most? Why?
- Were there any judgments or evaluative statements made?
- If so, how can they be avoided in the future?
- Were feelings or written facts discussed?
- Did the conference include praise or blame?
- Was the feedback specific?

- Did the coach's questions lead the teacher to draw conclusions?
- Did the coach become too directive?
- Would notes or audio recording or video recording have been better?
- Were the facts gathered and presented in a nonevaluative manner?
- Will the process lead to the improvement of instruction?
- Will the teacher act as a coach?
- Will the teacher request another observation?
- Who—teacher or coach—benefits the most from Peer Coaching?

In my experience, this last question produces both answers until the participants begin to think about the true beneficiary—the student. Peer Coaching does improve instruction by refining the dissecting skills of the coach and teacher, but any discussion of instruction results in increased learning for the student in the classroom.

A SAMPLE DIALOGUE FOR THE PROCESS REVIEW

Barbara the Coach: "Okay, now that we're finished with that step, let's do the Process Review. Let's look at this list. Who talked the most?"

Buddy the Teacher: "Well, I believe I did. I did not hear you make any evaluative statements, but I made a couple."

Coach: "That's okay if you make evaluative statements. You are supposed to analyze your lesson. Did we discuss feelings or facts?"

Teacher: "We talked strictly about facts, and I don't remember any praise or blame during the talk. And all the facts you gave me were directly related to my specific request. You did not get off the focus. Your questions forced me to draw my own conclusions. You made me dig."

Coach: "Did I become too directive as coach?"

Teacher: "No, not at all. But you know, I'd like to try video taping so I can look at it several times as I plan for higher-level questions and improving my delivery."

Coach: "Do you think this process will improve instruction?"

Teacher: "Yes, I think I showed me that I'll have to keep working on equity."

Coach: "I think I learned about equity from coaching this lesson."

Teacher: "I definitely will ask you to come back to coach, and I would be glad to coach you. I learned a great deal about my own teaching, and I think my students will benefit."

Coach: "Well, I think I learned from having to refine my listening and coaching skills. I will be a better teacher after having coached you. But I agree, the students will benefit because we will both improve instruction."

CHAPTER 9

Selling and Buying into Peer Coaching

SELLING PEER COACHING TO THE SCHOOL BOARD
AS AN INVESTMENT

With all the money that schools and districts have invested in staff development over the last five years, how many of those dollars have proved to be sound investments? How many of the innovative programs are still present in schools? Districts and schools can save money and ensure that staff development will work using the research base for the program outcomes and the actual experience of a district or school that has implemented the program. In other words, get programs that have worked in similar districts.

The very best use of district and school staff development dollars is on teacher training, teacher coaching, and user-friendly maintenance. Dollars need to be spent on getting individual teachers to internalize new skills. A process that will do that in-house is necessary instead of depending on people who are not in school every day such as consultants and district staff. Peer Coaching is such an in-house structure and process. It can become so much a part of the daily routine of a school that teachers will put it on as comfortably as an old pair of shoes.

A good example of investing staff development dollars in-house comes from Marshall Elementary School in Orangeburg, S.C. Principal Geb Runager decided that instead of hiring a Student Team Learning consultant from Johns Hopkins to come in to train his forty-two teachers in that cooperative learning program, that he would send John Young, his fourth-grade teacher, to Hopkins to be trained as a national trainer. Then Young would come back to Marshall Elementary, train all the teachers, and still be there to provide refresher courses, coach, and problem solve for STL. The staff development dollars were the same, but Marshall bought an in-house trainer instead of buying the time of a training consultant who would return to Baltimore.

If schools or districts combine each new staff development program with training in Peer Coaching, they buy security for their investment by knowing that teachers will help each other internalize and maintain the skills. New programs are more likely to realize their full potential if teachers are helping each other daily with practice and implementation. Using Peer Coaching in the school eliminates the dependence on outside people to maintain the innovation.

In their research on the coaching of teaching, Joyce and Showers (1983) have found that one-or two-day workshops do not provide enough time to develop the degree of competency necessary for most teachers to be able to apply a new skill in the work setting. They maintain that at least fifteen or twenty practices are necessary to gain control of a moderately difficult skill.

How does a school or district get a teacher to practice the new skill fifteen or twenty times if the teacher has to wait for a principal or an outside observer to help with practice? The discouragement factor operates here because the teacher must wait for coaching, depending on the principal's or outside trainer's schedule. If the coaching does not take place immediately and in the workplace, teachers give up trying to practice the new skill. As soon as the staff development training takes place, teachers must begin practice in the workplace with a peer on hand to provide coaching. If a school has Peer Coaching in place, then each new content or methodology staff development program will automatically have a process to assist the practices necessary to internalize a new skill. District and school staff development dollars will have the insurance of Peer Coaching.

Bacharach and Conley's 1986 research on organizational behavior found that any authentic professional development program should focus on the expansion of teaching skills. Peer Coaching provides a teacher with coaching on a particular skill from the new program, but it also provides the coach with reflective and analytic skills necessary to grow as a professional.

It has also been suggested that training time for any professional development be organized so that 40 percent of the time is spent on generic skills, 40 percent on concrete experiences, and 20 percent on worksite coaching.

How does this compare with the prevailing system? In our fifty years of experience in education across six states, Buddy and I have seen quite the opposite. What we have seen in twenty nationally recognized staff development programs in which we have trained is that 80 percent of them spend 100 percent of the time on generic skills. Almost none deal with concrete experience in the classroom as part of the daily practice and implementation because of the problems with scheduling outside observers. We have seen no time allocated for coaching except for the coaching we have done in our own schools and as trainers. Considering this allocation of time, is it any wonder that most of the training time and dollars have been wasted?

For those interested in wise investments, Peer Coaching is not only efficient but also cheap. Once trained in Peer Coaching, teachers, principals, and trainers can use it to implement and maintain the content of any staff development program. An entire Peer Coaching episode is time-effective also because the entire five steps can take as little as thirty minutes in a teacher's working day. Therefore teachers can use Peer Coaching every other day to reinforce newly learned practices or improve instruction. If Peer Coaching is in place, future staff development dollars will not be wasted because the structure will be in place to continue learning generic skills through concrete experience and Peer Coaching.

Dollars can also be saved if we use Peer Coaching to maintain or shore up existing staff development programs that may be floundering. For instance, in South Carolina, ninety of the ninety-one districts invested heavily in the Program for Effective Teaching, a variation on Hunter's effective teaching model. In the state's version, maintenance depended on district office observers and principals. Through no inherent fault of their own, these outside observers could not be in the classroom often enough to help teachers internalize these new skills. Because of this scheduling and frequency factor, many effective teaching skills did not get the fifteen or twenty practices necessary for mastery. Peer Coaching helps alleviate these types of problems because the teacher-to-teacher coaching can take place almost daily.

One outside observer working with fifty teachers to coach new skills usually can schedule four visits per teacher per year. This falls way short of the necessary fifteen to twenty practices needed for mastery of a new or moderately difficult skill. If, however, twenty-five of the teachers are using Peer Coaching at least once a week, that means 750 coaching visits in-house. That number could allow for the fifteen or twenty practices needed for mastery.

Another dollar factor for schools and districts is the retention of quality teachers. We have known for years that teachers do not enter the profession to make money. Dedication and service has been the motivating factor for the brightest and best, but we continue to lose them because of job dissatisfaction. As teachers move up the staircase of personal needs, they move closer to self-actualization through job satisfaction.

Maslow's hierarchy of needs begins at the lowest level:

1. Physical safety
2. Shelter and clothing
3. Acceptance
4. Self-esteem
5. Self-actualization

Placing emphasis on Peer Coaching will help ensure that schools and districts meet the job satisfaction needs of the quality teachers and keep them in the district. As the district gains a reputation for meeting the higher professional needs, it will have fewer problems attracting and keeping quality teachers. This saves the taxpayer's dollar by spending less on recruiting and getting the most for the dollar due to the experienced quality teachers in the district.

This is a wise investment of taxpayer money for even the steely-eyed business accountant. What business would turn down an investment in experienced teachers that kept paying a dividend year after year? What business could turn down the chance to give workers more satisfaction and increase production? What business would not rejoice in reducing turnover and the necessity of training new recruits year after year? This will help alleviate one of the chief reasons that quality teachers leave the profession. We often forget that highly dedicated quality people always need chances to grow professionally. Since they are not in education for the money anyway, they will leave if we do not provide chances to grow. Peer Coaching professionalizes teaching, which in turn leads to greater job satisfaction.

John Halfacre, an outstanding principal in South Carolina, uses the practitioner's logic as a reason for spending time and money on Peer Coaching. Halfacre brought Peer Coaching to his school because he reasoned that if it does nothing else, it will increase the time that teachers spend talking about instruction. They have to discuss the lesson in the Request for the Visit. Teacher and coach must reflect on instruction during the Visit and the coach's review of the notes. Active engagement, talk, and sometimes argument about instruction is natural during the Talk after the Visit and also in the Process Review. In using Peer Coaching, the teacher must spend at least thirty minutes weekly in structured talk about instruction.

Since there is a correlation between time on task and student learning, one could draw a logical conclusion that the more time teachers spend on task discussing improvement of instruction, the greater the benefit to students. Increasing the time spent on discussing instruction produces more of a chance that quality instruction will occur. Quality instruction results in students achieving at a higher level.

In some classrooms, the mere fact of having another teacher visiting frequently improves the learning climate. The less-effective teacher may teach differently with more frequent observation. Affective if not cognitive learning will improve. Being observed by a peer often stimulates a higher level of teaching than is possible in an isolated situation with a closed door.

The poor teachers are not the only ones who need observation. The excellent teachers benefit even more from coaching. Just as Olympic divers get better as each performance is coached, so teachers need to use coaching. My experience as a trainer has been typical. Although I have had many years experience as teacher, principal, and trainer, I found that my skill level increased incredibly as I added coaching as a regular part of my professional practice.

In summary, Peer Coaching saves the district's investment in staff development by providing a maintenance system to:

- internalize new skills
- reinforce existing skills and practice
- tap previously untapped resources for observation
- use district personnel more effectively
- increase dramatically the observation of instruction

Recruitment and retention are less of a problem for the district because quality teachers are offered more job satisfaction.

CHAPTER 10

Putting Peer Coaching in Place in a School

How do I get Peer Coaching started in my school? Can you give me a time line? Can I turn the implementation over to teachers? How much money will it cost? Who does the training? Will I train small groups of teachers first? How structured does it have to be? Do all my teachers have to coach? What will the outcomes be for teachers? For students?

These are practical, everyday questions that the reader may have at this point. The purpose of this chapter is to answer in commonsense terms these and other questions about how to implement Peer Coaching in the workplace and address problems that may arise during the early stages of implementation.

Implementation consists of six sessions:

1. Selling Peer Coaching
2. A training session in five steps
3. Practicing Peer Watching
4. Skills needed to peer coach
5. Troubleshooting
6. Peer Coaching

SESSION ONE: SELLING PEER COACHING

The first session on implementation takes about one hour but it is critical. It requires a little background work by the salesperson. The leader should read the Peer Coaching book and be familiar with the research. About a week before the hour-long session, each teacher should be given a copy of Joyce and Showers's article on "The Coaching of Teaching." This home-work should whet the appetite, give the teachers a preview, or at least pro-voke some interesting questions.

This session is held in an area where participants are seated in groups at tables. It begins with the leader giving the participants a writing prompt that elicits thoughtful reflection. The writing prompt is "Staff development is. . . ." Each person is to write and complete the sentence honestly for about two minutes. Then the leader says, "Discuss this definition in your groups for about five minutes." After about five minutes, the leader asks groups to share definitions and writes some on chart paper for the group to see.

Unless your group is the rare exception, most of the comments will be negative. Then the leader asks the group to list six or seven staff development programs they have attended during the last few years. The leader asks the group how many of the programs they have tried initially and how many of them are still in use. The group then identifies the reasons why such a small number of innovative practices is still in use.

The leader next defines staff development and the importance of transfer. If staff development does not transfer to the classroom, it is useless. This is a good time for the leader to compare what happens with trainer and teachers with what happens with teacher and students in the classroom. All of our work in lesson planning and new ideas will be of little use in the classroom unless students use them. The same thing holds true in a staff development training session. If the trainer has a great program but no teacher uses it in the classroom, the training is useless.

Using the listed reasons as a springboard, the leader relates the lack of usage to the Elements of Teaching Chart and the percentages researched by Joyce and Showers. Ask the group how much each remembers from a college lecture course that was all theory. As they all remember very little, the leader can begin by saying that theory alone can produce only 5 percent of new skills. The leader then explains the chart and the importance of all five elements in learning.

If the leader has a skill to illustrate the five elements, he or she can dramatize the point. For example, one trainer uses juggling three objects. He explains the theory of juggling three objects. He then demonstrates how to do it. Each person takes three objects and tries to juggle them, then gets feedback on the juggling. The trainer assures them that they can learn to juggle if they have continuous support and coaching with their practice. Most agree that they cannot do the new skill after theory, demonstration, and one practice.

In order to present a mental and visual picture of transfer, the leader can demonstrate a physical skill such as roller skating, a dance step, Chisanbop math, playing a C chord on a guitar, or whistling a tune.

The leader at this point will discuss the advantages of Peer Coaching and the professional development it offers. The teacher can use Peer Coaching for a new technique, a new skill from staff development, or a problem or concern in classroom instruction or management.

The second half of this overview session consists of defining Peer Coaching, listing the five steps, and modeling them.

The leader should define Peer Coaching and list the five steps with a brief explanation of each. The transparency and handout master "Peer Coaching: Five Steps" can be used here. Two people then model the five steps in Peer Coaching using twenty to thirty minutes for the whole process. The leader may choose to list the five steps without modeling and save the demonstration for the next session, which is a full day of training. She may use the scripted dialogue in the book. The leader should model the role of the teacher since it is important that the leader be perceived as a recipient of coaching. Teachers should see the principal as one willing to be coached.

The session should end with a preview of the next training session in which participants will receive full training and two practices, one as teacher and one as coach. Teachers should bring any concerns they have about this new process to the next session.

SESSION TWO: TRAINING SESSION IN FIVE STEPS

About a week after the overview session is held, the leader conducts a full training day for the five steps of Peer Coaching. A brief review of the definition, the Elements of Teaching chart, and the five steps of Peer Coaching are used to begin the session. The leader then answers the teachers' concerns about beginning Peer Coaching.

Next, the leader discusses the role of the principal and the role of the teacher in Peer Coaching. The five steps of Peer Coaching are then discussed in great detail, with the checklist in the hands of the teachers. Teachers are encouraged by the fact that they can use this checklist as they begin using Peer Coaching.

Two persons then model the five steps. A selected group of the participants act as the students in the model lesson, or the whole group may act as the students for the lesson to be coached. Step Three, the Coach Reviews the Notes and Lists Possibilities, is the only silent step and is difficult to model. The trainer playing the coach must think aloud to illustrate the thought processes for this step. I have found that using an overhead projector to write down the leading questions and the suggestions helps the audience visualize the process.

At the end, the leader answers questions about each step and emphasizes why certain restrictions such as "No praise, no blame" are used. This part of the training can be enhanced if the two persons who model the steps videotape this lesson. Teachers can play the tape later for reinforcement as they begin to use Peer Coaching. This part takes from one hour to ninety minutes.

The next step moves us from modeling to guided practice. In this part of the training, the teachers actually role-play a selected problem by using all five steps. Each teacher has a chance to practice both the role of coach and the role of teacher. To accomplish this, the two trainers must be prepared to teach three additional lessons no more than ten minutes in length. In my experience, I have found that adult learners pay more attention to model lessons that are *not* related to school curriculum. Some of the effective lessons I have used are new learning for adults:

- How to Remove a Fishhook from Your Arm
- Learning the Quarterback Stance
- How to Distinguish Fingerprints
- Cross Country Snow Skiing
- Hand Gestures for the Hula
- Steps in Clogging
- How to Program a VCR
- How to Jump Start a Dead Battery
- How to Tie a Non-Slip Knot
- How to Use Korean Finger Counting Math—Chisanbop

The leader arbitrarily divides the group into trios. Each trio decides who will play the roles of coach, teacher, and process observer in this first practice. The two trainers define the problem by modeling the first part of the Request for the Visit. They define the problem and the type of data collection to be used. The pairs (teacher and coach) then role-play the remainder of the Request for a Visit, using the checklist. The process observer reminds the pair if they have forgotten any part of the checklist. This takes five to ten minutes.

Directions must be clearly and simply stated for Step Two, the Visit. One of the trainers must teach a model lesson. The trainer must have students. The persons role-playing the teachers will act as the trainer's students during this Step Two only. Following the model lesson, these "students" will then resume their role as teachers.

In my experience, I have found that this part of the Visit may require several explanations. Patience is necessary because teachers are not accustomed to assuming very active roles in staff development.

The leader asks each trio to identify the person who is playing the role of the teacher. This can be done by raising hands or passing out buttons with the word "teacher" or "coach" on the button. One trainer then teaches the lesson with the "students" as his class.

The people who are role-playing coaches gather the data using the previously agreed-upon format. The trainer not teaching the lesson should walk around the room and make sure that the coaches are taking notes. This may sound simplistic, but I have found that many people get so caught up in the lesson that they forget to take notes. Then they have nothing to discuss for Step Four, the Talk after the Visit.

Because the coach needs five to ten minutes of silence to review his notes and list possibilities, the teachers and process observers take a break and refrain from talking to the coaches. The trainers walk around the room, assisting the coaches with analyzing the data, writing leading questions and listing suggestions on a separate paper. Each coach should also practice the opening statement for the Talk after the Visit.

The trios regroup for Step Four, the Talk after the Visit. The coach and teacher role-play this step using the checklist and the data gathered during the model lesson. The coach carefully makes the opening statement, "Remember you asked me to gather data on . . ." and then the coach and teacher perform Step Four. The process observer carefully notes any evaluative statements made by the coach. She also estimates the percentage of time each talks.

When the coach and teacher finish Step Four, the process observer reports any evaluative statements and the time percentages. The trio then discusses this report by the process observer. This step should take no more than ten minutes because people start talking about other things and lose the focus of the conference.

The leader or trainer at this point asks the whole group, "Who has the notes?" If the teachers have the notes in each trio, then they have paid attention to detail.

The trios complete Step Five, the Process Review, by asking each other the fourteen questions listed in that section.

This process will be repeated twice so that each person in the trio has a chance to play teacher, coach, and process observer. Each model lesson, with participants practicing all five steps, will take about forty minutes.

Since this is a long training day with active participation, trainers should remember to keep refreshments available at all times and to have frequent breaks.

Each participant should be given a reflective writing homework assignment. This helps each person reinforce in writing what happened during the session and what it means to her. This speeds up the desired internalization process. Their reflective writing will be shared at the next session. Some suggested reflective topics include:

- The things I liked most about Peer Coaching are . . .
- The things that might prohibit me from becoming involved in Peer Coaching are . . .
- The characteristics I will look for in a peer coach are . . .

SESSION THREE: PRACTICING PEER WATCHING

This session is approximately one hour long and has two purposes. The first is to discuss the reflective writing done by the teachers. The second is to outline the three phases of Peer Coaching and to set the stage to begin Peer Watching. Teachers in groups will spend ten minutes discussing their answers to the reflective writing question. The leader brings the group back together by sharing the findings in each group and listing some common concerns. The leader should openly discuss the concerns and ask for group wisdom on tough questions. The phases of Peer Coaching are:

1. Peer Watching
2. Peer Feedback
3. Peer Coaching

Each leader should begin by instituting Peer Watching for two months unless teachers in the school have visited in each other's classroom at least four to eight times during the past year.

To keep it simple, the practice of Peer Watching should begin with the leader assigning pairs to watch for four visits during a prearranged time and make note of the objective taught in the lesson. No comments should be exchanged, since our purpose is to get teachers accustomed to visiting in other classrooms.

A team of teachers can keep track of the progress of Peer Watching by asking each teacher to turn in a simple record slip giving the name of the two teachers, the date, and the lesson observed.

SESSION FOUR: SKILLS NEEDED TO PEER COACH

This is the fourth training session, which should take about three hours. The group attending this session will be potential coaches. With a faculty of fifty teachers, the leader might do this session with 15 to 20 percent of the teachers. This group consists of those outstanding teachers who always look for ways to improve their excellent teaching.

Understanding the difference between feedback and coaching is essential to institutionalizing Peer Coaching among the teacher population. In other models of coaching that involve supervisors, feedback and coaching are considered the same thing. To build confidence among teachers who are learning to peer coach, a simple progression from merely handling the data (feedback) to offering suggestions for improvement (coaching) must be a carefully considered step.

Since this is a reflective model instead of a technical model, expertise and comfort must be built gradually. Feedback is the coach presenting to the teacher the information collected on the teacher's Request for a Visit. In feedback, a mental image that will help focus the coach is to say to himself, "I am a camera." The feedback is void of any of the coach's personality or comments: no evaluative statements and no directive statements. The coach should be Joe Friday on Dragnet, "Just the facts, ma'am!" No head nods and no body language should be given by the coach to convey approval or disapproval of the teacher's lesson.

I have found that this part of the training—to begin with feedback before true coaching—is the most difficult for teachers. We have to overcome the natural tendency which supervisors and evaluators have used for years. They have been trained to say something positive for even the worst lesson. Teachers are smart, however: they wait for the "but" and for the other shoe to drop.

It is very important that no part of this model be evaluative. Even the traditional warm fuzzies or token opening positive comments are evaluative. Just getting and giving feedback is a paradigm shift that will require a period of adjustment and deliberate thought. Potential coaches must spend a great deal of time practicing this skill.

The only way to acquire this skill is to practice feedback by Peer Coaching's rigid rules. This initial session consists of guided and independent practice of feedback skills under the leadership of a trainer. The group should again be divided into trios. The practice can be handled in several ways: in-baskets, video lesson, or simulated lesson.

One method is to prepare in-basket sheets that contain the Request for a Visit and sample data collections. Each trio then performs Step Four of Peer Coaching with coach, teacher, and process observer roles. The process observer stops the feedback whenever evaluative statements are made, no matter how minor. The action is also stopped when the coach gives head nods or any body language that conveys approval or disapproval. The leader walks around to observe any evaluative statements and body language in the trios.

The second method uses a previously videotaped lesson that includes the teacher's Request for a Visit and the lesson in question. All three persons in the trios take notes on the videotaped lesson. Each in turn plays the role of coach delivering feedback to a teacher with a process observer. Again the process observer and the leader watch and listen for evaluative statements and body language. The advantage of three people delivering feedback on the same lesson is to examine and practice all variations.

The third method to practice feedback with potential coaches is for the leader to present a live lesson including a Request for a Visit. Again each person gets to practice collecting data and playing the role of coach delivering feedback.

At the end of this session, the whole group lists the most difficult aspects of delivering feedback. This list must be discussed by the group before moving on to true coaching. The whole group then practices giving feedback four times in the workplace during the next two weeks. Potential coaches should observe and practice with each other.

After two weeks, the group reassembles for training in true coaching skills. The session opens with discussion of the practice during the past two weeks and the difficulties encountered. The leader redefines the difference between feedback and coaching.

During this session, the leader will discuss coaching skills:

• body language
• active listening
• observation skills
• adult roles

The leader begins this part by asking everyone to freeze. With humor, the leader asks each person to describe the body language of persons in their trio. The trios discuss how they read body language of other people. The leader may dramatize the situation with exaggerated body language during this time: looking at the clock or watch constantly, getting behind a desk or table in a defensive position, or shuffling papers instead of making eye contact.

Defining the importance of body language, the leader discusses the research or message analysis. Body language gives off overt and covert signals which may destroy the meaning of our words. Advertisers have found that 78 percent of any message is visual, 13 percent is voice tone, and only 9 percent is the words themselves. You can see this by watching any television ad. The same percentages apply to everyday messages inside and outside the workplace.

The leader demonstrates receptive body language and closed or negative body language. Very briefly, the leader gets the group to mimic an example of each. For practice, the group divides into pairs. One person starts talking about what happened yesterday. Her partner uses exaggerated negative body language. Then the partner switches to receptive body language. Afterwards the speaker discusses the effects of both types. Then the pairs switch roles. This practice should take about ten minutes.

Although we do not deal extensively with body language, potential coaches should consult books on the importance of body language in business and teaching.

The next hour of this training session is devoted to active listening skills. In this reflective model of Peer Coaching, it is very important that the teacher do most of the talking in the Talk after the Visit. The leading questions assist in this process, but the coach must learn the value of silence and active listening skills. Traditionally we recognize that high verbal skills are characteristic of teachers. The hard part is learning to use silence. We have a tendency to fill up any void with sometimes meaningless talk. Silence makes us uncomfortable.

To start this section, the leader can dramatize the effect by standing and remaining silent for one whole minute. The leader asks the group for their reaction to the silence. He correlates this with wait-time from the staff development program called Teacher Expectations, Student Achievement (TESA) and with the questioning part of Hunter's model of effective teaching. Wait-time is also important in teaching higher-order thinking skills or problem solving. Teachers learn to model thinking time and effective pauses and silences. The leader may dramatize this by asking everyone to remain silent for two minutes, think, and maintain eye contact with people in your group. Since we find this strange, people may start to laugh and be unable to keep silent for the two whole minutes.

The recommended books for active listening are Thomas Gordon's *Parent Effectiveness Training, Teacher Effectiveness Training,* and *Leader Effectiveness Training.*

How to Gather Data

Another skill taught during this training session is how to design data gathering devices. Simplicity is the key in gathering data during the Visit. Two teachers can develop data gathering devices that will fit the concerns they want observed without any elaborate forms to follow. The best data gathering devices are those designed by teachers to meet their particular concern for observation. KISS (Keep It Simple, Stupid) is the rule of thumb. The two teachers may start with a simple tally or chart as they begin Peer Coaching. As they get more comfortable and skilled in the process, their data gathering devices get more complex while they attack more complex concerns.

The next step may be to practice listing verbatim questions during the lesson with the student names attached. If total script taping is the desired data collecting device, I advise videotaping the lesson or practicing script taping two minutes during the evening news.

Teachers often complain that the problems addressed in the Peer Coaching training are too simple for their needs. In dealing with adult learners, however, what we are trying to teach is the process of Peer Coaching. The process is learned more easily if the model problems are kept simple. As teachers become more comfortable with the process, then they can handle more complex concerns inventing their own ways to gather data. That is why there are no data gathering forms in this book.

Adult Roles

Another skill to be taught during this session is recognizing adult roles. Popular psychology has taught us a great deal about the games people play in their jobs and in their social lives. This phenomenon was best described by Dr. Eric Berne in *Games People Play.* His discussion of the roles we play in different situations helps us a great deal with the Peer Coaching situation.

Dr. Berne describes three roles that we assume in our interaction with other adults. The two roles we play every day are child and adult. In most situations between adults, very seldom do we have adult-to-adult roles. One person normally assumes the role of child and the other the role of adult. One may play many roles during the day or the same situation. Traditionally a teacher assumes the role of child when dealing with a supervisor who enacts the role of adult or parent. Even in later years, at family gatherings, the baby sister is always the baby sister even if she is in her sixties. A principal in Peer Coaching training related the following incident. She was advising her twelve-year-old about what he should do. Things got hot and heavy when the son vehemently argued with his mother. Shouts ensued. The mother got into a shouting match with the child. The son told his mother, "I hate it when you get down on my level." This is a good example of the adult assuming the child role in the situation.

The ideal solution, according to Berne, is that in any situation, both adults should play the role of adult. In Peer Coaching, this means that the coach must always play the adult role and never treat the teacher as the child role. Even if the teacher tries to assume the child role, the coach must bring the Talk after the Visit back to the adult level.

Despite the value of body language, active listening, and adult roles, the most valuable training for coaching is drawing on years of experience. In this reflective model, when given the opportunity to reflect on experience, most coaches find that they have a vast array of skills and knowledge. This process forces us to bring to a conscious level and think about skills and knowledge that we have never had the time to use. With this time to analyze one part of a lesson, pairs of teachers have time to talk about skills that may be extraordinary.

Madeline Hunter has said that we know more about teaching than we actually use. The problem is bringing all that skill and knowledge to a conscious level. This reflective model of Peer Coaching forces us to take the time to do this in structured ways.

Another aspect of this kind of coaching between teachers is that one does not have to have all the answers. One of the good parts about this kind of coaching is that it allows teachers time to sit down and problem solve together using their own expertise and wit. An outcome of adults using it may be the two teachers doing research in libraries, talking with other teachers, or experimenting with different possibilities in the class-room. Peer Coaching provides a support system for isolation among teachers because it really gives them a structure to discuss instruction.

An interesting exercise at this point is for the leader to ask each teacher in the room to write a number summarizing the total years of experience each has had in education. Ask each group to add up the years and then total them for the entire group. One session included teachers with 640 years of experience. That number will focus attention on the value of teacher talent and expertise or at least on the ability to engage in mutual problem solving.

A reflective list might be solicited from the group of the characteristics of a good peer coach. Some might be confidentiality, good listener, professional, honest, admits that he does not have all the answers, willing learner, deals in facts instead of feelings, avoids personalities, is organized, is not afraid of silence, risk taker, innovator, always looking for a better way, enjoys working with people, and open-minded. While these are characteristics of a good coach, they are also characteristics of a good teacher or leader.

The group of coaches should be sent out to practice their new coaching skills with each other for four weeks. Eight visits should be exchanged. Following each visit, the process review should include writing down problems or concerns for Session Five.

SESSION FIVE: TROUBLESHOOTING

The troubleshooting session begins with discussion of written problems and concerns during the four weeks of practice coaching. The leader takes time to deal with any situational concerns openly and honestly. Ask coaches to reflect on skills such as body language, active listening, and the adult role. A five minute reflective writing exercise at this point gets the participants to write about how their coaching during the previous four weeks has influenced their teaching. Group discussion follows the writing exercise.

In order to renew the original concept, two trainers will then model the five steps of Peer Coaching with an extremely difficult situation. A complex Request for a Visit and a teacher who resists during the Talk after the Visit are two difficulties to model. The resistant teacher will continually ask how he did or how the coach liked the lesson or will refuse to self-analyze or talk.

Following the modeling of the five steps, the trios are presented with another complex in-basket Request for a Visit, along with the data that they must role play and analyze. If the trainer wishes to give the coaches opportunity to practice in a complex situation, then a model lesson should be taught. Each member of the trio takes a turn being the resistant teacher. Practicing responses to the resistant teacher will take fifteen or twenty minutes.

This part of the renewal session takes approximately forty-five to sixty minutes. The next two hours of this session is a decision-making process to develop a plan for implementing Peer Coaching in the school. This will include structure for all faculty to enter Peer Coaching, numbers involved, times, phases, and keeping track of Peer Coaching sessions. The results of this session should be taken to the entire faculty for discussion.

SESSION SIX: PEER COACHING—SHOW TIME!

Peer Coaching can be started in mixed assigned pairs, within departments, or within grade-level teams. Some of the faculty can work in pairs, some as department or grade-level teams, or some in mixed teams. Each group should have at least one trained lead coach who has been through all of the extra training. The groups should include only six to eight people.

The group should do Phase One, Peer Watching, for two months or four visits. At least Peer Watching should be required of all faculty. The group should use the Peer Watching form to keep track of the visits. The form reports only the names of the two teachers and the date. No designation is made of who is the watcher and who is the teacher observed. One teacher in the group should collect the forms. The group should meet for discussion at the end of two months. Next the group enters the Peer Feedback phase and does this for two months.

Four Peer Feedback Visits should take place during these two months. During this phase, each coach should have a fellow coach serve as process observer during the Talk after the Visit. The group reconvenes for discussion of practice and problems at the end of two months.

After four months of practice with Peer Watching and Peer Feedback, the group is ready for Peer Coaching. Failure to observe this gradual introduction to Peer Coaching will severely hamper internalizing true Peer Coaching. What we are really doing is changing the school culture by reducing isolationism, promoting collegiality, getting teachers into each other's rooms, and increasing the amount of time professional educators spend discussing instruction. Any dramatic cultural change needs time and careful nurturing.

Up to this point, many of the concerns have been simple so that teachers could internalize the process of Peer Coaching. As we enter real-time Peer Coaching, school-wide problems might be addressed by all coaching groups. For instance, let's say teachers have just completed training in TESA (Teacher Expectations, Student Achievement). As the teachers begin to implement TESA, each department or grade-level team will use Peer Coaching to assist in planning, supporting, deciding appropriateness, and giving feedback and coaching on the TESA skills.

A second example concerns using disaggregate analysis. Each department or grade-level group identifies which race, sex, or socioeconomic status group is achieving at an unacceptable rate. The department chooses teaching strategies that will perhaps work for the low-achieving students. Peer Coaching will be used to plan, support, decide appropriateness, and give feedback and coaching on the observed use of the group's strategies.

A third example of Peer Coaching implementation concerns improving an existing program. For instance, suppose *Math Their Way* has been used in the school for several years. The coaching group can observe each other teaching the program. Feedback and coaching can be used to identify problems and share effective practices. As new strategies are developed, each teacher can be coached on adding them to his repertoire.

The faculty started with 20 percent involved as specially trained coaches. As the faculty becomes more comfortable with Peer Coaching, the leader trains more coaches. The ultimate goal is to have every teacher trained as a coach.

Like fine wine, Peer Coaching improves with age. The more teachers use this process among themselves, the better they get at being observed and coached. Peer Coaching stimulates innovation, identifies unrecognized problem areas, creates a demand for more specialized training, increases collegiality in a restructuring school, and increases time spent discussing instruction. Ultimately Peer Coaching ensures that more skills are transferred to the classroom so that students can benefit.

The benefits of Peer Coaching are not limited to the teacher population. Trainers, principals, superintendents, district office coordinators, and directors can all use Peer Coaching to improve their job performance. Coaching is appropriate for principals' meetings and staff development training.

I have learned always to train in pairs. All of my training sessions and presentations are coached. Even if one partner is doing most of the talking, the other partner is always there to assist and coach. Coaching is such an integral part of my training that my coaching partner and I automatically sit down at the end of every session and coach each other. We are so addicted to the coaching element that we do not consider any training session complete until we have done our own Peer Coaching.

I recently asked Dr. James Jennings to coach for clarity of directions in a complicated training session. Roland Barth, author of *Improving Schools from Within* (1990), was keynote speaker for a week-long training that included Peer Coaching. Dr. Jennings and I described our process of coaching each other. Barth demanded that two people observe and coach his presentation to one hundred principals. He asked that his feedback and coaching session be conducted in front of the entire group. This vivid example of the importance of Peer Coaching opened the minds of the principals.

Peer Coaching is not limited to the five steps in the original structure. When Peer Coaching partners have reached a level of professional confidence with each other, they may vary the process. For example, in one seminar, Jennings was teaching entirely to the left while ignoring the right side of the room. At the first break, I said he needed to include the right side of the room. The change was immediately apparent. Between us, the two hand signals—"time out" and the throat slash for "cut it!"—have been lifesavers. "Real time" coaching is a logical next step. The coach can give nonverbal feedback during a lesson or training seminar if both parties agree. The real-time coaching can also take place as professionals coach each other on lesson or unit plans or during team planning time. This must take place in a culture of renewing trust between teachers. These are all examples of extensions and variations of Peer Coaching among professional educators.

Instituting change will always be met with resistance whether it is part of a reform movement or an isolated innovation. Some of the resistance is contrived and well-organized, but most of it is a natural human reaction to the change process. Research says that people are more comfortable dealing with what they know even if it is not productive. They are more comfortable with old habits even if we can prove to them that the new ways are better. The collaborative approach used by Peer Coaching goes against the grain in a culture that for decades has encouraged isolationism and not sharing. Because of this, those planning to institute Peer Coaching must have as part of their plan how to deal with resisters.

Managing and planning change is one of the strategies necessary for any innovation and the larger reform efforts. According to Shirley Hord (1987, 1991), leaders can expect teachers to fall into one of six categories as they deal with any change, including Peer Coaching. There will be 8 percent who are innovators who will try any proven innovation. About 17 percent are leaders who will organize the training and implementation, pass out the forms, and begin scheduling the time. About 29 percent are willing to adopt the change once the selling job has been done by the leaders. They are the early majority. About 29 percent will adopt the change if they see their peers successfully using it. They are the late majority. Resisters number about 15 percent: they will refuse to change their old habits until the flood over-whelms them. In any group, the leader can expect about 2 percent active saboteurs. The best strategy for them is to ignore them.

It is pointless to waste 80 percent of our energy on the 17 percent who are resisters and saboteurs. If the leader spends 80 percent of her energy on the majority who will implement Peer Coaching or any other change, the program will be more successful.

At the Center for School Leadership, we believe that managing change is the most vital generic force. We deliver a three-day seminar in Manag-ing Change each month for teams of teachers and administrators from the restructuring Associate and Partner Schools. With a 99 percent success rate, this seminar has enabled schools to handle change and to set in mo-tion many other innovations with less faculty resistance.

If the leader prepares people for generic change and then follows with a selling job on the benefits of Peer Coaching, then follows the simple five steps of Peer Coaching and the guidelines provided, the process is straightforward. Teachers need to have meetings to explore and discuss the need for Peer Coaching. They need to have teams and support groups in place for this or any other innovation. These teams should discuss, in-quire, redefine, and modify the Peer Coaching process in the school once people are comfortable with the concept. Remembering that the relation-ships among the adults in the school determines the model for student achievement, teacher teams should continue to modify Peer Coaching to their own needs.

I have seen evidence in schools that if these five steps and guidelines are followed, Peer Coaching can be successfully established as a col-laborative model. It must be nurtured in a culture that encourages trust and collaboration.

CHAPTER 11

Teaching Portfolios and Peer Coaching

THE RELATIONSHIP BETWEEN PEER COACHING
AND TEACHING PORTFOLIOS

Peer Coaching can indeed stand alone as a collegial process for improving instruction without the taint of supervision or evaluation. Teachers can also, in a more realistic sense, incorporate the process as a "value added" documentation of their greater professional commitment to the analysis and improvement of instruction into peer review team processes and the increasing use of portfolios.

Artists and architects have traditionally presented their work in portfolios, and now that custom is becoming a part of a teacher proving himself a master of his profession. Two important trends in teaching portfolios will be discussed in detail in this chapter to demonstrate the important contribution that Peer Coaching will make to documenting analysis and improvement of instruction. The first is the National Board for Professional Teaching Standards and its requirement for a reflective portfolio as part of the criteria for national certification as a master teacher. The other requirements include a videotape of instruction and an exam. (For more information, contact the Board at its national headquarters in Southfield, Michigan, which can be reached via <http://www.nbpts.org>, by phone: 248-351-4444, by fax: 248-351-4170, or by mail at National Board for Professional Teaching Standards, 26555 Evergreen Road, Suite 400, Southfield, MI 48076.)

The second is a discussion or adaptation of the process of a teacher creating her own portfolio for evaluation. This adaptation is based on my own experience in creating a teaching portfolio. A long-overdue and welcome innovation is using teaching portfolios instead of campus politics for college decisions for promotion and tenure. As a college professor in 1996, I engaged in the process of creating a teaching portfolio for a tenure and promotion process. This discussion adapts the key points of that ex-

perience to the needs of K–12 classroom teachers who are preparing portfolios for evaluation. This portfolio format can be used for enhancing ordinary evaluation decisions, for evaluations such as peer review teams,
and for state-mandated teacher evaluation such as the ADEPT and TEAM
processes in South Carolina.

PORTFOLIOS FROM THE NATIONAL BOARD FOR PROFESSIONAL TEACHING STANDARDS

In Spring 1990, Joe Delaney, a district superintendent, and I were appointed by the South Carolina Department of Education to represent the
state on a national task force headed by North Carolina's Governor Jim
Hunt to set national teaching standards with a national exam and national
certification for master teachers. Most memorable about the task force
meeting in Chapel Hill was the guest speaker, son of two teachers, Coach
Dean Smith. As an educator properly awed by a childhood hero, I mingled
around with the other teachers and government officials at the reception
in the Dean Dome. Delaney, knowing of my hero worship, urged me to
meet Coach Smith at the door and ask for his autograph. Thinking this
celebrity autograph hunting was beneath the dignity of the august company assembled, I was embarrassed and hung back until I saw people bar-
ing arms and holding out pieces of clothing for the great coach to autograph. His speech was memorable for teachers because he said that he was
grossly overpaid and that teachers like his parents and all teachers were
grossly underpaid. The weekend ended with a down-home pig-picking
hosted by Governor Hunt, who made sure that all guests received a sou-
venir red bandanna.

From that enlightening beginning, field tests were conducted in several
test states by what became known as the National Board for Professional
Teaching Standards (NBPTS). South Carolina became a field test site, with
the University of South Carolina as the testing agent. Advisory Board members were appointed from a cross section of groups representing teacher in-
terests. As executive director of the South Carolina Center for the Advancement of Teaching and School Leadership, I was an advisor for policy, testing,
and support of candidates. From the initial group of applicants who completed the process, six teachers from the state earned national certification
during the first round.

The process for national certification, at least in that first round, involved an intensity never experienced before by teachers and subse-

quently discouraged many who were indeed master teachers but could not complete the process. One of the candidates was a middle school teacher from Lancaster, S.C., who had been in one of my graduate classes in supervision and evaluation. She found it difficult to teach full time, to work on her portfolio nights and weekends, and to borrow computer time, since neither she nor her school had a computer for her to use. It is hard to imagine now six years later that a master teacher might fail national certification for lack of a computer, but then it was a very real possibility. Despite many difficulties, including paying her own fees, she was among the first six in the state to earn national certification.

In addition to passing a national exam in the teaching area, the NBPTS required candidates to submit a classroom video and a teaching portfolio. The heart of the portfolio consists of reflective commentary by the teacher to think through instructional practice and analyze his effectiveness. Excellent teachers analyze instruction every day in order to increase student learning, but the intensive reflection required by the NBPTS can inspire a teacher to monitor and manage student learning in a more precise way.

Using the NBPTS portfolio criteria as the bridge, one can see the immediate connection with Peer Coaching. If a teacher were preparing a portfolio to document excellence in teaching for national certification, it would be easy to produce that required reflective commentary to analyze his effectiveness in modifying instruction to increase student learning. The process that other professionals engage in by enlisting the assistance of a peer is evident as a surgeon invites a peer to assist in the surgery or to analyze a problem or an attorney rehearses her closing statement with a colleague.

Working alone on intensive reflection on instruction practice, a teacher can meditate and contemplate the very subjective question often asked by supervisors to begin evaluation conferences: "How did you *feel* the lesson went?" As we have indicated repeatedly in Peer Coaching, feelings are not the primary goal when analyzing instruction. Instead of working alone on her intensive reflection concerning instructional practice, the pragmatic teacher working on his portfolio for National Board certification will demonstrate her (1) cooperative work with professional colleagues and (2) adoption of the research-based Peer Coaching as an analytical system for her reflection.

Using Peer Coaching instead of writing about his solo musings on the improvement of instruction can be impressive in constructing a portfolio, but it can also save time and effort in the documentation. If a teacher seeking National Board certification uses Peer Coaching as the device for intensive reflection, the documentation can be records of a series of Peer Coaching sessions. Two scenarios can illustrate the difference.

In the first scenario, the teacher prepares a lesson for his American government class on checks and balances among the three branches. He has five elements in his lesson: a homework assignment for background reading in the text, a fifteen-minute lecture, twenty minutes for learning teams to prepare their response to a checks-and-balance problem, ten minutes for each of five teams to present their responses, and five minutes of summary by the teacher. Later that day, the teacher reflects alone or with a video tape of the lesson and records his impressions of what was successful in the lesson, what was not successful, and the points at which non-success could have been changed to success. Was his lecture clear and sequential from concept to topic? Was the problem for the learning teams directly related to the lecture and within their capacity to solve? Were all members of the learning teams participating? Were the presentations to the point? Was the teacher's five-minute summary a doorway to further understanding?

Even as he composes his analytical reflective piece concerning the lesson, he is still seeing it with his eyes only. He is analyzing student reactions with the eyes and mind of their teacher: one who knows them from 180 days of class time, one who never discounts personalities or previous circumstances from the lesson, and one cannot separate data from feelings.

Scenario two takes us into the systematic use of Peer Coaching for analyzing instruction and improving the intensive reflection required for a National Board portfolio. The teacher plans the same lesson in American government with reading assignment, lecture, a problem for learning teams, presentations, and teacher summary. But instead of reflecting on his instruction alone, he has engaged in the Peer Coaching process:

1. He asked a colleague to coach him during the class. The teacher asked the coach to gather data on his transition between the lecture and assigning the problem for the learning teams.
2. The coach visited and gathered data in the form of notes on the teacher's lecture conclusions, the directions for the problem, the student reactions, the students' engagement in the task within their learning teams, and the teacher's summary.
3. The coach reviewed her notes and listed three suggestions or questions for transitions and clarity.
4. The teacher and the coach met at the end of the day. The coach reviewed the data with the teacher. The teacher made some comments about the clarity of his observed directions to the learning teams. The

lack of connection between the student presentations and the teacher's summary immediately struck the teacher. He made some judgments himself on the lesson that were apparent from the data collected with another pair of eyes and hands. He was quite ready for the three suggestions his coach had prepared.

5. In the review process, the teacher and the coach could discern that they had looked at the problem and the data with an absence of *feelings*. They had both used the data to analyze the lesson to find the point at which the lesson could be improved.

After this Peer Coaching session, the teacher who is preparing a portfolio for the National Board can more easily document his intensive reflection on the improvement of instruction. A series of Peer Coaching sessions involving this problem or this concept will be even more impressive. The actual notes and conclusions from the session can be written with an introduction and reflection on how the process of Peer Coaching has assisted the teacher in analyzing and improving instruction.

One can see how scenario two presents a more professional and systematic analysis. It also demonstrates to the National Board that the teacher is engaged in long-term analysis and improvement of instruction because this Peer Coaching process is clearly no one-shot deal with him. The second scenario also illustrates that the teacher is actively engaged in working with professional colleagues for the improvement of instruction.

Perhaps not every teacher will be a candidate for National Board certification and find the Peer Coaching process easy to document analysis of instruction, but every teacher will sooner or later encounter an evaluation system, such as TEAM in South Carolina or peer reviews in other places, which will demand that the teacher analyze her instruction for improvement.

A TEACHING PORTFOLIO FOR EVALUATION

As a college professor, I required portfolios from my students in courses such as "Introduction to Professional Education" and "Tests and Measurement." Freshmen who began their education majors with the introductory course also began the rudiments of a four-year portfolio. Two of the important sections included (1) essays on teaching and (2) a plan for taking required and nonrequired courses, as well as summer and part-time jobs in education-related fields. The essays on teaching included "Why I Decided to Enter Teaching" and "My Philosophy of Teaching." The latter essay was clearly understood to be the preliminary draft of an essay that would develop through many courses, all four years, and the teaching internship. This freshman portfolio would also become the basis for the student's graduating portfolio, in which the chief focus would be the teaching internship. Most seniors could and did use the portfolio for job interviews.

The portfolio I required my students to make in "Tests and Measurement" was a reflective writing portfolio, which set the model for later reflective writing on analyzing and improving instruction. My design for "Tests and Measurement" included four distinct sections per class period: lecture, a problem to solve by learning teams, solution presentation, and instructor's summary. The course was also divided into three types of work related to each topic in testing, such as selected response items, interpreting standardized test data, computing standard deviation, or disaggregate analysis of test scores for equity.

The three types of work per topic included test making, test taking, and test analysis. Instead of outlining the chapter for homework to prove that they had read the material, the students were required to make a short test using the most important ideas from the chapter. Many times, the next class began with students exchanging papers and taking another student's test. The built-in peer review, peer critiquing, and peer pressure that resulted from this device produced interesting learning. As the course progressed, more complicated test items were required. After the class session on the particular topic with the four divisions indicated above, students took a test of the instructor's making, just as teachers and students have traditionally been engaged in learning first, then test taking. However, the third type of work around a particular topic increased the student learning exponentially. Before the scored tests were handed back, each student wrote an essay critiquing the teacher-made test. They could analyze each item type for bias, clarity, adherence to Popham's rules, and level of Bloom's taxonomy.

The student portfolio for "Tests and Measurement" consisted then of each student's first constructed test, her best test, her best analysis, her mini-lesson and the resulting test, and her reflective essay on the progress of her learning. The portfolio experience cemented for many students the learning from the course.

This end-of-the-course portfolio began to take hold among education faculty as a good collection of course learning and reflective writing. My aim was to see the freshmen constructing introductory portfolios, seniors presenting job portfolios after the teaching internship, and each worthwhile education course resulting in a portfolio of the student's learning and reflective writing on the subject. Dr. Nancy Beede's student portfolios for the "Exceptional Child" and Dr. Ann Ishler's student portfolios for "Student Teaching" were outstanding examples.

Obviously, education faculty were well acquainted with the content and reflective writing portfolios when, in 1996, college faculty were invited to attend a seminar in creating teaching portfolios based on Peter Seldin's *Successful Use of Teaching Portfolios* (1993). The driving idea was to educate a portion of the faculty in teaching portfolios so that the Tenure and Promotion Committee could make better decisions about promotion and tenure that were based on actual accomplishments instead of on campus politics, favoritism, or seniority.

During the workshop, faculty members constructed portfolios according to the nine criteria set up by Seldin:

1. Statement of Teaching Philosophy
2. Rationale for Teaching Portfolio
3. Teaching Responsibilities
4. Analysis of Methods and Strategies
5. Description and Study of Course Materials: Syllabi, Assignments, Handouts, Realia
6. Efforts to Improve Teaching: Conferences, Workshops, Curricular Revisions, Experiments in Pedagogy and Methodology
7. Student Ratings
8. Teaching Goals: Short Term and Long Term
9. Appendixes

All of these criteria, except student ratings, are easily adaptable to K–12 teaching and the construction of teaching portfolios. The student ratings category and the ratings themselves should probably be eliminated from colleges except those which are entirely dependent on tuition for funding.

In section four, Analysis of Methods and Strategies, I can demonstrate my writing excellence by intensive reflection on the analysis of instruction. Or I can demonstrate that I am not afraid of inviting a colleague into my class to help me analyze my methods and strategies using the systematic process of Peer Coaching. My peer coach can help me analyze the written plan, the students' reaction, and the clarity with which I present or try new methods.

Seldin's sixth category is the crucial category for the use of Peer Coaching. Conferences and workshops can be worse than useless in most efforts to improve teaching, unless the study is systematic and the results of research and best practice are consistently applied in the classroom. Curricular revisions are fine for improving teaching on paper and in catalogs, but revisions seldom have any relationship to improved teaching within the curriculum. The section on experiments in pedagogy and methodology, however, allows the excellent teacher who is constructing a portfolio an obvious place to document Peer Coaching in the improvement of his teaching.

This scenario illustrates my adoption of the Learning Styles program known as 4 MAT by Excel Corporation. Peer Coaching makes it possible for me to incorporate my new learning into my teaching methodology. After seventeen days of seminars (not a conference or workshop), I planned lessons in the four quadrants to reach all learners. Since I am a Global Four learner whose mask has been Traditional Two learning, it is important that I as a teacher plan to reach learners in quadrants one and three: interpersonal and results-oriented learners.

I request a visit from a colleague who also knows the 4 MAT learning cycle and ask him to observe my use of methods in one lesson to reach learners in quadrants one and three. The coach visits my classroom and takes notes on the teacher's introduction, set, discussion directions, and group summary. He also notes the interaction (or lack of it) among the students. The teacher's set for an analogy to the learning topic is particularly difficult for me, but the coach duly notes the teacher's set and the students' actions. The coach decides that analyzing quadrant one learning is enough for one session and leaves. He reviews his notes and prepares for the Visit. Since both of us are veterans of the seventeen days of seminars, we can use the same vocabulary in discussing my ability to reach all learners with quadrant one techniques and strategies. I am ready to hear all of his suggestions for improvement as long as they are couched in "No Praise, No Blame" terms. We review the process and decide to repeat the quadrant one observation two or three more times before going on to my quadrant three strategies.

The simple five-step Peer Coaching process in this scenario has done more to improve my teaching than simply stating in my portfolio that I have "experimented with new techniques and methodologies." How is anyone to know whether the new techniques worked or not unless I have a peer coach? Are my solitary musings on my experiments valid documentation? Do I try three new methods on my own, decide that none work, and go back to my lecture-test-lecture methods?

Documentation of several Peer Coaching episodes or a series on the same topic therefore makes it easy to show the teacher's efforts toward improvement of instruction. It is hard to see how another method of documenting improvement of instruction could be as valid as Peer Coaching.

A report from another set of eyes and ears—those of a knowledgeable professional colleague—is a much less subjective documentation than a solitary teacher analyzing his own instruction. Even in analysis and formal reflection, the solitary teacher still sees the lesson with his own eyes and hears with his own ears. He cannot be objective about the effectiveness of his teaching or about the efficacy of the students' interaction with the learning. Peer Coaching solves that solitary dilemma.

For Seldin's other eight sections, the criteria can easily be adapted to the K–12 teacher who is constructing her own portfolio for evaluation. The statement of teaching philosophy is one of those things we have all done as college seniors; but as master teachers with years of experience, this section becomes the cornerstone for all that follows. As an example, I am including part of my own statement because I firmly believe that consistent use of lecture is detrimental to teaching and learning:

My Teaching Philosophy

Basic to my teaching/learning philosophy is that all persons should be continually engaged in learning, especially teachers or those committed to education. The particular emphasis in my present undergraduate teaching concerns the preparation of future teachers. Even at the pre-professional level, I firmly believe that all teaching and learning is a matter of choice and decisions. If a student has a serious commitment to becoming a teacher, even at the sophomore level, it seems to me that my task is to provide information and experiences that will prepare that person to be the ideal teacher.

If the person does not have the serious commitment to the profession of teaching, it is my task to provide him with the options to make the decision to become serious.

My philosophy of teaching and learning involves setting up for students a list of concepts necessary for a particular domain. Within each concept, I aim to provide basic information in the form of new facts that relate to their current experience so that they can frame the new learning with connections to their present experience. I aim to make the new learning cohesive in short, concise logical sections.

Immediately after presenting new concepts to form new synapses so that students can connect the new learning to their personal experience, I like to present an application level problem for them to solve using their personal experience and the new learning. My belief is that if a skill or piece of knowledge is not applied immediately then it does not get transferred from the student's short term memory to long term memory.

My philosophy of teaching and learning includes as one of its primary elements the fact that students can reinforce their new learning best by practicing
it with peers. In all my teaching career—high school English, kindergarten,
second grade, fourth grade, undergraduates in education, graduate students in
supervision, teaching incumbent principals and teachers, and now again in
graduate education—I have formed learning teams to review and practice the
new learning I bring to students. The focus of learning teams is peer pressure
and learning from peers; but the emphasis is on "each one teach one," that one
never really absorbs any learning until he teaches it himself. The teacher has a
crucial role while learning teams are functioning inside the class: to make sure
that erroneous learning is not occurring. It is my task to circulate constantly
among learning teams in this section of my teaching to correct errors and to set
students back on the correct path. One must be very careful so that dominant
members of learning teams do not persuade others to errors.

The final part of my philosophy includes active participation on the part
of every student, in learning teams and in Socratic questioning and discussion with the whole class. Despite avowals of shyness on the part of recal-
citrant learners, it is my firm belief that future teachers must learn by active
participation, first in small learning teams and eventually with large groups.
It is also my belief that learners of all types, whether future teachers or not,
must actively participate in constructing their own meaning in learning.
Analogies and stories are an important part of constructing meaning but so
are discussion and critiquing with and for peers.

Seldin"s second section, Rationale for Teaching Portfolio, allows the
teacher to reflect on why this intensive analysis of her reason to be will
display to herself and others her excellence in teaching. A teacher's pas-
sion and commitment to his profession is made clear in this section of systematic thought and planning. This section can illustrate his philosophy
for learners, just as section one illustrated his teaching philosophy. Section
three allows the professional teacher to align her assigned responsibilities
with her assumed responsibilities in order to justify her time to herself, her
evaluators, and her family.

Section five allows the creative teacher to shine. He can show innovation in his outline of the course and his creativity with real artifacts, assignments, and handouts. The excellent teacher will also use this section
to show how she uses learning teams, student discussion, student projects, and learning styles to reach all learners. Including copies of tests
that accurately measure the learning he has constructed is something that
only the best teachers can do. If he can demonstrate that he measured
learning with other valid and reliable devices, he is certainly ahead of the
game.

Section eight is the place where the master teacher stretches herself to the edge of her learning. She illustrates that her mastery of teaching is conditional upon continuing to learn herself. From brain research, we know that dendrites dry up without water, but synapses also become slower if brain cells are not constantly exercised to fire rapidly and connect to old learning. Short-term goals may apply to this year's continual improvement efforts in instruction, but long-term goals may include new areas of learning to master, new degrees, or new skills to incorporate.

The appendixes can include documents that support the portfolio. These eighteen appendixes were included in my college teaching portfolio: Syllabi, Letters from Colleagues, Nominations, Curriculum Revision, Master's Design, Design Teams, Alliance of Educators, Grants, Student Samples, Transparencies, Video List, Handouts and Realia, Learning Teams, Student Portfolios, National and State Involvement, Scholarship, Areas to Improve, and Publications.

Typical documents for the K–12 teacher might include items such as these from a Columbia College professional development school teacher:

Letters from supervisors and colleagues
Letters from students and parents
Nominations
Staff development: participant and leader
Curriculum design teams (or grade level)
District participation
State/national participation
Extracurricular
Community outreach
Outlines of courses
Transparencies and handouts
Video list
Computer and Internet projects
Artifacts
Real-world expeditions
Student samples
Teacher-made tests
Standardized test results
Scholarship: books and articles read and/or written, courses
Grants
Team work
Areas to improve and strategies

For those interested in further discussion, models, and critiques of teaching portfolios, e-mail the author at <bgott@earthlink.net>.

SUMMARY

Portfolios from the National Board for Professional Teaching Standards

Like most policy makers in education, I fervently hope that national certification becomes the standard to replace state-by-state certification and the myriad of tests and measurements now in place. Using Peer Coaching to document improvement of instruction by analysis and reflective writing is an important part of a teaching portfolio, whether or not the requirement for national certification ever becomes a reality.

If our goal is a competent teacher in every classroom, national certification is a lofty goal—coupled, of course, with salaries to match. Naturally, reaching this goal is interwoven with many changes, including reforming teacher preparation, examining the tax base for school funding and teacher salaries, and making teaching a profession like medicine instead of the service organization it is in many places now.

A Teaching Portfolio for Evaluation

By studying teaching portfolio models and books such as Seldin's *Successful Use of Teaching Portfolios*, each classroom teacher can learn to construct a teaching portfolio for evaluation or promotion. Peer Coaching is an essential ingredient in documenting "Experiments in Innovative Pedagogy and Methodology" and "Improvement of Instruction." Documenting efforts to improve with Peer Coaching episodes is more sensible than listing attendance at a weekend education conference. Excellent teachers have always collected scrapbooks or notebooks of their teaching, but now the time has come to formalize these efforts as professionals who use factual documentation and Peer Coaching into professional teaching portfolios.

CHAPTER 12

Next Steps: Changing Teacher Preparation and Evaluation Systems

INSTITUTIONALIZATION OF PEER COACHING

Teacher-to-teacher Peer Coaching remains the most valuable application of this technique. In schools where all interested teachers had participated in the seminars on an equal basis, Peer Coaching is most successful. Teachers learn the simple, five-step process and begin using it on their own. They are peers and build trust over time and with the strategies listed in this book. Peer Coaching is less successful when the administrator picks an "elite" group of master teachers who become "peer" coaches and "do it" to the un-picked groups of teachers. It is also less successful (as in Charleston), when the administrator sets the schedule for coaching sessions or keeps control of coaching schedules by hiring a floating substitute for a day for everyone to be coached on that day. Teaching is a variable succession of decision making: I may not need coaching on a day (e.g., Thursday at 10 A.M.) when the floating sub is scheduled for me!

Peer Coaching works best when teachers build trust with each other, set their own schedules, and use Peer Coaching on an almost daily basis. Teachers as real peers have control of time, place, and subject. It is used by request to improve teaching, with no "elite" team, no administrative schedules, and no reporting to administrators. Peers coaching each other works best.

Administrator-to-administrator coaching works on the same basis. When peers—administrators, superintendents, district office personnel, staff developers—build trust, learn the simple, five-step approach, and use it daily, Peer Coaching works best.

Community groups have also used Peer Coaching in public meetings, at church budget groups, at decision-making teams, in presenting a new program, or announcing new information to the public. PTA–PTO presidents have used it within executive council meetings and with the membership, especially when difficult votes are before the group.

TEACHER EDUCATION TRIADS

College faculty have begun to use Peer Coaching in minuscule amounts. Faculty across campus interested in innovation in teaching or collaborative learning or peer support have met in groups to learn some basics. Faculty pair off and try to observe each other at least once a month. The mixture has been interesting: a test and measurements professor observing a children's literature teacher, a sociologist observing a physical education instructor, a special education faculty member observing a math professor. Teacher-to-teacher Peer Coaching has been difficult to implement in colleges because of some professors' definition of academic freedom and the typical isolation with which college teachers surround themselves.

A more enlivening example occurred when I was state site director (1991–98) for the Goodlad Initiative in South Carolina. Five colleges had formed a collaborative and were selected as the eighth national site when John Goodlad formed his National Network for Educational Renewal in 1991. Benedict College, Columbia College, Furman University, the University of South Carolina, and Winthrop University were—and are—the five collaborating colleges. Each college pledged to establish Professional Development Schools in which to place their teaching interns and by 1998 had established forty-two professional development schools.

At Pontiac Elementary School, a version of triad coaching took place. A college professor who was broker or liaison with Pontiac as a Professional Development School (PDS) taught a graduate course in conceptual science to eight Pontiac teachers at the school site on Wednesday afternoons. The college teacher modeled each new concept. On Thursday morning, each teacher implemented the new concept in his or her own classroom with the student teacher and the college teacher as coaches. Then the student teacher would teach a lesson using the concept with the college teacher and classroom teacher as coaches. Of course, a great deal more learning and modeling took place than these simple steps indicate, but the model Peer Coaching for Triads was also begun at the University of South Carolina at Aiken and at Columbia College with its ten professional development schools.

Peer Coaching for Triads involves a professional model of demonstrating and learning teaching strategies and classroom management that could replace the traditional college courses if classroom teachers were willing to be partners in training teaching interns and if college teachers were willing to put their skills on the line. In the traditional model of student teaching, prospective teachers take general education courses for two years. Lecture, note taking, and testing are the three models of teaching which future teachers learn from many general education professors. During sophomore and junior years, future teachers are assigned to field experiences or clinicals in which they act as teacher aides or observers. They sink or swim with no real supervision, selection of exemplary teachers, or outline of skills to learn and practice.

During junior and senior years, future teachers take methods courses which are at times little more than "cut and paste" making of kits and games with no real experience of learning theory or styles. Education professors also use the lecture-notes-test style of teaching. They may lecture on cooperative learning or discovery, but seldom if ever use or model these innovations, which are common in classrooms. After learning "methods" from the traditional lecture model and perhaps teaching one "mini" lesson to classmates at the end of each course and turning in a "portfolio" of cut-and-paste artifacts, future teachers are turned loose in the classroom to work for a cooperating teacher, again with no outline of skills or advanced learning theory and again with very little supervision. After twelve weeks, the student can become certified to teach in his or her own classroom.

Using Peer Coaching for Triads as a model for educating future teachers, taking time for modeling skills and assigning deliberate reflection on skills would replace clinicals and the worst features of methods courses.

In learning to teach science, the future teacher would study content and a vast repertoire of techniques to teach science (or any subject): cooperative learning, learning styles, discovery, discussion, lecture, experimentation, community projects, and so forth. The courses (science content and science methods) would be taught on site at a local school (preferably a PDS with the college and a long relationship of trust). This would ensure the student teacher has familiarity with lab equipment typical of public schools and that the student learned specific techniques from the classroom teacher and the college professor.

The triad—classroom teacher, student teacher, and college professor—would meet to discuss each new concept as it was introduced. The classroom teacher would model-teach the concept to demonstrate expertise in teaching method, and the college professor would demonstrate the concept in the classroom to add depth of knowledge and variety of technique to the teaching. The student teacher would teach the concept to demonstrate a beginning expertise in both content and method. After each concept, the three people would reflect and discuss the lesson using the rules of Peer Coaching.

Like the pairs in true Peer Coaching, the triad could each learn from one another to improve his or her own teaching. It is interesting to observe student teachers model lessons and being coached. It is rare to see a classroom teacher model a concept and submit to coaching by a "peer"—college professor or student teacher. It is unique to see a college professor teach a lesson or concept in a school classroom and then sit down as equals with the classroom teacher and the student teacher to be coached. But why not? If all three stick to the simple rules of Peer Coaching, observe the "No Praise, No Blame" rule, and act like professionals, each could improve his teaching and the learning of his present and future students.

A MODEST PROPOSAL

Like Jonathan Swift, I make a modest proposal stemming from my twenty-eight years in education in various aspects of the system from student to teacher to state director to college professor:

1. Abolish the tenure system.
2. Change the way teachers are trained.
3. Set one firm measure for teacher evaluation: each student reading on grade level.
4. And, of course, motivate all teachers to use Peer Coaching to improve teaching and increase student learning.

Tenure

In our decades, women are not limited to nursing, teaching, or secretarial work because the opportunities are unlimited. We are not talking here about equal pay or the glass ceiling, but merely the opportunity to enter any career. It is my firm belief that teachers should be evaluated on job performance like people in other jobs.

Part of the recommendation to abolish tenure would, of course, be more than adequate resources to do the teaching job properly. If the incompetent teachers were eliminated from the system, however, public money would flow more easily to the competent teachers who produced competent students. Competent students who could fill out a job application, read and write an analysis of an article in any given magazine, and work with people on a team would also change citizens' attitudes toward public education.

Change Teacher Preparation

An undergraduate who plans to be a teacher has the same need for a liberal arts education as any student in the first two years of college. He should be well-grounded in math, English, humanities, sciences, arts, and literature. He should be taught by master teachers (professors) who have current knowledge and model ideal teaching skills themselves. What he is taught should radically change during his junior and senior years.

During her last two years in college, the future teacher would ideally be taught theories of teaching and learning, brain function and hemisphericity, learning styles, and diagnostic analysis instead of the many memorize-the-text or make-and-take courses she now takes. She should learn the science of teaching with all the theory, research, and background just as if she were preparing to be a rocket scientist or a foundry worker. As Ron Edmonds said: "We now know all we need to know about teaching. The only question remaining is why don't we use what we know?"

The turf wars of college education departments should not be allowed to continue to produce mediocre student teachers who sink or swim in their first years of teaching—if they last that long. The proliferation of courses is one way to insure college professors' jobs, since unfilled classes are not usually continued even for tenured professors. (Of course, I believe that tenure should be abolished for college professors also.)

The Peer Coaching system should, of course, be mandatory for teacher interns after or during their learning of theory, brain function, learning styles, and diagnostic analysis. Internship in an exemplary public school would allow a true apprenticeship for the future teacher and allow classroom teachers some skilled assistance for no additional money. Having learned the science of teaching in the college classroom, the future teacher needs to learn the art of teaching on the job as an apprentice in the public school. Peer Coaching for Triads is part of this art of teaching. For any given concept, any member of the triad should be able to plan, teach, be observed and coached, and teach better.

Peer Coaching triads are composed of classroom teacher, teaching intern, and college education or arts and sciences professor. Whether the concept is subtraction in Chisanbop math or hypothesis proving in earth science, any member of the Peer Coaching triad should be able to teach the concept, be coached on the art/science of teaching, and teach better the next lesson. The classroom teacher could be the first rotation, teaching a concept. The teaching intern and the college professor would both observe and coach. The teaching intern would, of course, benefit most from teaching a concept and being coached. Or would he? Could all three learn from observing and coaching each other? Could a college professor possibly learn a new technique from a public school teacher or a teaching intern?

As we learn in Peer Coaching for pairs, the coach often learns more than the teacher! Aha! Then the college professor takes her turn at demonstrating a lesson that furthers the concept with the classroom teacher and the teaching intern observing and coaching her. Learning the art of teaching as part of a Peer Coaching triad would improve the training of a teaching intern, but it would also improve the skills of the classroom teacher and the college professor. The college professor would be compelled to put her skills on the line along with her assurance of theory. The classroom teacher would find it stimulating to explain why he chose a particular strategy in relation to learning theory or brain function or learning style.

As in Peer Coaching for pairs, this system of Peer Coaching triads would certainly improve the skills of the three professionals; but more importantly, it would increase the learning of all their students.

Each Student Reading on Grade Level

Reading is a basic tool for success in all subjects, as well as being essential for life skills. It would be ideal if we could expect all students to be at grade level (whatever that is) in all subjects, but graduating eighteen-year-old students who are able to read and analyze a magazine article is a high goal to aim for in our present system. All students reading on grade level next year is impossible, but, like the district in California that bought computers for every student, it can be phased in year by year. Imagine this: next year all first graders would be able to read on grade level. All school efforts and resources would be concentrated on that one goal. In two years, all first and second graders would be able to read on grade level. In twelve years, all first through twelfth graders would be able to read on grade level.

One measure—students reading on grade level—could be used to evaluate teachers. The expense would be far less than the present system. By any chosen measure, can your students read on grade level? If yes, you have a job for next year. If not, you are fired. Find another job. If that were the only measure, perhaps teachers could find the time, ingenuity, science, art, skill, computer, phonics or whole language—any strategy the teacher could find—as long as his students were reading on grade level by the end of the academic year.

Compare this with other jobs for a reality check. Saleswomen: reach a set quota in sales or you're out. Rocket scientists: make this Saturn rocket blast off successfully to install a new satellite or we find another rocket scientist. Police dispatcher: respond to 911 calls effectively or be assigned to drive a school bus.

Use Peer Coaching

The last part of this modest proposal is indeed modest. I have studied or observed or participated in twenty-three models of "peer" coaching. All of them involve a level of supervision, whether it is blatantly a supervisor coaching or a cadre of trained elite who are the coaches for their "peers." Even in the most effective models (other than true Peer Coaching), training some teachers as coaches and not others automatically puts them off the level of peers with classroom teachers and onto the level of supervisors, no matter that they are called peer coaches.

For even peer review teams to work effectively, a change in the environment of schools is necessary. That necessary environmental change could be effected by Peer Coaching. Months, nay years, of opened classrooms, Peer Watching by pairs of teachers, Peer Feedback among colleagues interested in improving teaching, and true Peer Coaching among trusted and trusting professional peers can lead to the point where peer review teams—real peers, not the same old administrators with a teacher-of-the-year thrown in for sweetener—can work as an evaluation tool.

APPENDIX 1

MASTERS FOR HANDOUTS
AND TRANSPARENCIES

PEER COACHING:

A staff development model that

• provides a safe structured framework for a professional to observe a fellow professional

• provides feedback in five easy steps.

USES OF PEER COACHING

Peer Coaching will

1. help establish a line of communication among faculty.
2. provide teachers an opportunity for reflection and reflective discussion about their lessons.
3. help bring techniques teachers use instinctively to the conscious level, thus improving the chance that they will be repeated.
4. expand teaching skills by expanding coaching skills.
5. increase the amount of time teachers spend on discussing improvement of instruction.
6. provide adult interactions for teachers often isolated without adult feedback.
7. provide feedback on methods and pedagogy from respected peers.
8. improve teaching skills of coaches since they often learn as much or more by observing than being observed.
9. offer administrators a way of getting more people involved in the improvement of instruction.
10. help professionalize teaching since Peer Coaching offers teachers a chance to be involved in instructional decisions that impact them and their students.

BACKGROUND AND PURPOSE OF PEER COACHING

Morris Cogan's original work in clinical supervision in the Newton School System in 1973 began the idea of professionals helping each other. Robert Goldhammer also did major work at Harvard University in clinical supervision. Resident Supervisory Support for Teachers, an NDN program for staff development based in Washington, D.C., continued elements of clinical supervision. All of these, however, include supervision, evaluation, and judgment.

The present model, entitled Peer Coaching, had little in common with the previous models. It is based on the theory from Joyce and Showers and the practice of observing in the Effective Schools Training. In order to eliminated any vestige of supervision, evaluation, or judgment, a new model was designed in 1987 by Dr. Barbara Gottesman as the concluding module in the Effective Schools Training. The evolution of that model over the years has resulted in an independent staff development model used by schools, colleges, and collaborative organizations.

To avoid any connotation of supervision or evaluation, this technique is called Peer Coaching. It involves teachers acting as peers and observers in order to improve their own instruction and classroom management and thereby increase learning for all students. Administrators support the program by endorsing and introducing the concept to the entire faculty and by providing training. The administrator may participate in Peer Coaching by providing released time, class coverage, and general support. Under no circumstances should an administrator engage in Peer Coaching with a teacher. Administrators can engage in Peer Coaching with peer administrators in conducting faculty meetings or training seminars when one administrator is "teaching" or presenting and the other administrator is acting as coach to the presentation.

All professionals—doctors, lawyers, hairdressers, plumbers—get critiques by their peers in order to improve performance. Actors, dancers, and artists daily submit themselves to peer critiques to help them improve. All reform initiatives now include a leadership development component in which educators coach, mentor, or critique their peers. Ted Sizer calls this the "critical friend." Interdisciplinary units and new math/science techniques require peer coaches. Total Quality Management and systemic reform require that people coach each other and use teams for continuous improvement.

The model describes three phases: Peer Watching, Peer Feedback, and true Peer Coaching. The final phase, Peer Coaching, is a five-step process to provide teachers—at any level—with an easy structure for requesting and receiving a peer critique through a nonevaluative gathering of observed facts. The purpose of the model is to provide educators with the theory and guided practice they need in order to implement Peer Coaching in their own schools and colleges.

WHY PEER COACH?

1. Professional Needs for Growth toward Excellence

Peer Coaching:
- makes you examine your lessons in detail.
- gives you a chance to discuss your concerns with trusted peers.
- provides a learning experience by coaching in other classrooms.
- increases time spent on instructional improvement.
- makes teachers assume new roles and gives them a sense of empowerment.

2. Personal Needs

The teacher:
- gains adult feedback.
- develops support systems.
- improves collegial relationships.
- improves energy levels with renewal.

3. Institutional Needs: Schools, Colleges, Learning Organizations

Peer Coaching:
- improves the quality of instruction for all students.
- allows teachers to try out new ideas in a nonthreatening environment.
- helps identify areas of concern to lead to other staff development.
- increases the chances for transfer of learning.

TRANSFER/INTERNALIZATION
OF NEW SKILLS

When you add these five critical teaching compo-
nents, students learn, teachers learn, and administrators learn.

	Knowledge Level or Short Term	Application Level or Long Term
Theory	20%	5%
Demonstration	35%	10%
Modeling and Guided Practice	70%	20%
Feedback	80%	25%
Coaching	90%	90%

ROLE OF THE TEACHER

The teacher must:

1. commit to Peer Coaching to analyze and improve instruction.
2. be willing to develop and use a common language of collaboration in order to discuss the total teaching act without praise or blame.
3. be like Chaucer's clerke—gladly would he learn and gladly teach—to request observation and to observe as coach when requested.
4. be open-minded and willing to look for better ways of conducting classroom business. Excellent teachers always stretch beyond what they do now toward new learning to improve instruction.
5. act as a colleague and as a professional.

ROLE OF THE PRINCIPAL
OR ADMINISTRATOR

The principal or administrator must:

1. be committed to the concept of Peer Coaching.
2. establish new norms. The teachers are accustomed to being alone in their classrooms. The principal must sell the faculty on the benefits of visiting and observing in classrooms for the improvement of instruction.
3. provide structure during the early stages of Peer Coaching, at least for the first two months.
4. identify exactly what support will be given to teachers who use Peer Coaching.
5. provide time in the schedule and coverage so that Peer Coaching can occur.
6. generate outside support for Peer Coaching.
7. provide staff development for Peer Coaching and other training areas that may result from concerns in Peer Coaching.
8. validate the use of Peer Coaching in teaching portfolios.

Appendix 1

FIVE STEPS OF PEER COACHING

1. REQUEST A VISIT (5 minutes)
2. VISIT (10 minutes)
3. REVIEW NOTES AND LIST SOME POSSIBILITIES (5 minutes)
4. TALK AFTER THE VISIT (10 minutes)
5. PROCESS REVIEW (3 minutes)

PROCESS REVIEW:
CRITICAL DISCUSSION QUESTIONS

1. Who talked the most? Why?
2. Were there any judgments or evaluative statements made?
3. If so, how can we avoid them in the future?
4. Were feelings or recorded facts discussed?
5. Did the conference include praise or blame?
6. Was the feedback specific?
7. Did the coach's questions lead the teacher to draw conclusions?
8. Did the coach become too directive?
9. Would notes or audio recording or video recording have been better?
10. Were the facts gathered and presented in a nonevaluative manner?
11. Will the process lead to the improvement of instruction?
12. Will the teacher act as a coach?
13. Will the teacher request another observation?
14. Who—teacher or coach—benefits the most from Peer Coaching? (Trick question: The students benefit the most.)

CHECKLIST FOR THE FIVE COMPONENTS

1. REQUEST FOR A VISIT (5 minutes maximum)
   __ observation requested
   __ specific concern defined
   __ coach narrows concern
   __ confidentiality established
   __ no judgment or evaluation
   __ lesson to be observed
   __ data-gathering method, both decide
   __ seating chart, if necessary
   __ observer-coach seating or placement
   __ time/place
   __ time for Talk after the Visit

Notes:

CHECKLIST FOR THE FIVE COMPONENTS
(continued)

2. VISIT (10 minutes maximum)
   __ request written at top of page as reminder
   __ starting/ending time
   __ method to be used to collect data
   __ data collection on separate sheet
   __ no judgment or evaluation

Notes:

CHECKLIST FOR THE FIVE COMPONENTS
(continued)

3. COACH REVIEWS NOTES AND LISTS SOME POSSIBILITIES OR SUGGESTIONS
   __ coach reviewed data, deleted evaluation
   __ three leading questions listed on Coaching Form #1
   __ no judgment or evaluation
   __ suggestions listed on Coaching Form #2

Notes:

CHECKLIST FOR THE FIVE COMPONENTS
(continued)

4. TALK AFTER THE VISIT (5–10 minutes maximum)
   ___ plan where to sit in relation to each other
   ___ teacher or coach restatement of request in order to begin
   ___ stay away from "I" messages
   ___ coach goes over specific data collected and makes no outside observations
   ___ coach careful not to be trapped by teacher's comments like "What did you think of my lesson?"
   ___ ask three leading questions to analyze data collected on the specific concern
   ___ teacher analysis: get teacher talking
   ___ no judgment or evaluation
   ___ teacher request for coaching suggestions or alternatives
   ___ teacher request for further observation
   ___ coach gives teacher all notes or tapes
   ___ schedule another session or exchange

Notes:

CHECKLIST FOR THE FIVE COMPONENTS
(continued)

5. PROCESS REVIEW: DID IT WORK FOR US?
   (3 minutes maximum)
   __ teacher reaction to observation/coaching
   __ coach reaction to observation/coaching
   __ value of chosen data collection method
   __ conference strengths and weaknesses
   __ 14 Process Review Questions
   __ Who learned the most?
   __ Next session?

COACHING FORM #1

Request for Visit:

_____

_____

_____

Leading Questions:

1. _____

_____

2. _____

_____

3._____

_____

COACHING FORM #2

Suggestions for changes or improvements *when* the teacher requests them:

1. _____

_____

2. _____

_____

3. _____

_____

STEPS IN PEER COACHING:
A DETAILED GUIDE

STEP 1: THE TEACHER REQUESTS A VISIT (5 minutes)

A teacher requests a peer to observe a new technique of a single, specific concern in instruction or management. They set the date and time for the requested observation. Both agree on a data-gathering method such as writing down teacher questions/student responses or marking students called upon on a seating chart.

T: Purpose of the requested observation:
"I'd like you to observe my [new technique to be tried, practice of a learned skill, classroom management concern]."

T: Lesson or activity to be observed:
"Can you come to my class during [math, 5th period, etc.] to observe this specific concern while I teach?"

C: Date, time, and place for observation:
"Which day, time, and place shall I observe you?"
"Do I need a seating chart?"

C: How should the data be gathered?
"What would be the best way to record what I observe? Should I: make tally marks on a seating chart? use a stopwatch to count seconds of wait-time? write down your questions and students' re-

sponses? draw arrows on a seating chart to show your movements or proximity?"

T & C: Both decide on an appropriate data-gathering method.

STEP 2: THE VISIT (10 minutes)

The coach comes to the scheduled observation with an appropriate data-gathering sheet on which she has already written the teacher's specific request so that she can focus on his single concern. No judgment or evaluation statement is recorded. The time is recorded at the beginning, at intervals, and at the end of the observation.

C: Coach prepares data-gathering material beforehand.

C: Coach writes down the specific problem on which the teacher requested data or the new technique (such as question-pause-name) the teacher is trying.

C: Coach writes down beginning time.

C: Coach gathers data only on that specific problem or concern requested by the teacher.

C: Coach records data, leaving out any evaluation or judgment.

C: Time is marked or recorded in margins, if necessary.

C: Coach writes down ending time.

STEP 3: REVIEW NOTES AND LIST SOME POSSIBILITIES (5 minutes)

The coach reviews the teacher's original request for observation. The coach reviews the observation notes but does not summarize or categorize because the teacher himself must go through the raw data, step by step. The coach deletes any statements such as *Enough, Too much, Too little,* etc.

C: On Coaching Form #1, the coach writes down
     A. The opening statement for the Talk after the-Visit: "Remember, you asked me to observe your——?"
     B. Three or four neutral leading questions to keep the teacher talking and engaging in self-analysis of the lesson: "What does this data tell you?" *Never* say "How did you *feel* about your lesson?"
C: Coach reviews facts and clarifies any marks because the original notes will be given to the teacher.
C: Coach marks or numbers the specific facts or incidents. Coach may highlight categories or patterns, but it is better to let the teacher discover patterns.

STEP 4: THE TALK AFTER THE VISIT (10 minutes)
T: The teacher controls this conference, asking for the factual data gathered relevant to the specific request for observation. Either the coach or the

teacher restates the original request to begin the conference. The teacher looks at the data with the coach, talking through step by step. He analyzes the relevance of the data and begins drawing conclusions leading to solution of his concern. The teacher does most of the talking, asks for suggestions from the coach when he is ready, and may ask for an additional observation and coaching session.

C: The coach sits beside the teacher with the notes between them. The coach walks the teacher through each step of the data collected, letting the teacher do most of the talking, and asking leading questions to help the teacher arrive at his own conclusions. *The coach does not make evaluative or judgmental statements,* but the teacher may make evaluative statements on his own. Nonverbal behavior is very important here. Equal seating with the notes shared equally is an important factor to avoid the talkative supervisory stance of an evaluator. (Teacher leads, does most of the talking.)

T: Teacher restates request for observation: "I asked you to observe my. . . . What facts did you record?" Or the coach begins by restating the request.

C: Coach walks the teacher through specific facts from the notes and mentions times, if relevant.

T: Teacher listens to facts, talks about them, and states his own conclusions from the recorded data.

T & C: Teacher and coach reflect on recorded facts and their relation to the teacher's request for observation.

C: Coach may say, "What conclusions can you reach from these data that I recorded?" or "Are these enough facts to see the effects of the lesson?" or " Do you want me to observe this concern in another class or on another day?"

C: The coach *does not say:*
- I think the lesson was excellent.
- How did you *feel* the lesson went?
- Why did you do what you did?
- You should do it this way.
- I have the solution to your problem.
- Go and observe Mr. Goodteacher—he does this correctly.
- You need a workshop or course in——.
- You have nothing to worry about. Those kids misbehave in my class also.

T & C: If the teacher is ready for suggestions from the coach and indicates that receptivity, the coach consults Coaching Form #2. Rather than handing the teacher Coaching Form #2, she makes a suggestion from her notes and discusses it with the teacher. Other suggestions are discussed if the teacher asks for others.

STEP 5: PROCESS REVIEW: DID IT WORK FOR US? (3 minutes)

T & C: The teacher and coach analyze the process by asking themselves and each other a series of questions related to the method of data-gathering, the talking time of both coach and teacher, and the benefits of Peer Coaching to the teacher, the coach, the students, and the improvement of instruction. They should plan an immediate follow-up or set an appointment to reverse the roles, maybe on the same subject or concern.

1. Who talked the most? Why?
2. Were there any judgments or evaluative statements made?
3. If so, how can we avoid them in the future?
4. Were feelings or recorded facts discussed?
5. Did the conference include praise or blame?
6. Was the feedback specific?
7. Did the coach's questions lead the teacher to draw conclusions?
8. Did the coach become too directive?
9. Would notes or audio recording or video recording have been better?
10. Were the facts gathered and presented in a nonevaluative manner?
11. Will the process lead to the improvement of instruction?
12. Will the teacher act as a coach?
13. Will the teacher request another observation?
14. Who—teacher or coach—benefits the most from Peer Coaching?

THREE PHASES OF PEER COACHING

I. Peer Watching (2 months)
   A. Four visits to another classroom
      1. Noted on record
      2. No feedback
   B. Videotapes of self
      1. Four lessons taped and watched
      2. Four tapes erased

II. Peer Feedback (2 months)
   A. Training Session: Five Steps of Peer Coaching
   B. Coach offers no suggestions
   C. Four feedback sessions with peer, with no suggestions, just feedback of data

III. Peer Coaching (2 months)
   A. Review of Five Steps
   B. Coach offers suggestions when asked
   C. Four visits and four true Peer Coaching sessions

PEER COACHING EXCHANGES

Month 1 Dates:	**4 sessions**	**Teacher**	**Teacher**
	_____	_____	_____
	_____	_____	_____
	_____	_____	_____
	_____	_____	_____

Month 2 Dates:	**4 sessions**	**Teacher**	**Teacher**
	_____	_____	_____
	_____	_____	_____
	_____	_____	_____
	_____	_____	_____

Notes:

Most beneficial:

Barriers encountered:

POINTS FROM THOMAS GORDON'S
ACTIVE LISTENING

1. Avoid ordering, directing, commanding.
2. Avoid warning, admonishing, moralizing, preaching.
3. Avoid advising, giving solutions or suggestions.
4. Avoid lecturing, teaching, giving logical examples.
5. Avoid judging, criticizing.
6. Avoid disagreeing, blaming.
7. Avoid praising, agreeing.
8. Avoid name-calling, ridiculing, shaming.
9. Avoid interpreting, analyzing, diagnosing.
10. Avoid reassuring, sympathizing, consoling, supporting.
11. Avoid probing, questioning, interrogating.
12. Avoid withdrawing, distracting, humoring, diverting.

(from *Leader Effectiveness Training,* 1977)

For further study, consult Stephen Covey's *Empathic Listening.*

PEER COACHING: DOs and DON'Ts

DO
- Listen actively.
- Pause . . . and make reflective statements.
- Insert neutral probing questions to get the peer to continue reflection.
- Bite your tongue . . . and let the teacher talk.
- Let the peer fill the silent gaps.
- Review only the written data.
- Leave other concerns for another visits.
- Refer to the safety of the Peer Coaching rules.
- Offer to gather data using a different method.
- Lead into another visit or exchange.

DON'T
- Praise.
- Blame.
- Judge.
- Set yourself as an example.
- Offer solutions on your own not supported by research or practice.
- Fill silent gaps.
- Offer data that is not written as observed.
- Examine concerns that were not requested: offer no sidelines.
- Offer to break the Peer Coaching rules.
- Offer praise or blame: worth repeating.

PEER COACHING:
PRE-TRAINING AND POST-USE SURVEY

PRE-TRAINING

The survey should be administered before training or exposure to Peer Coaching.

POST-USE

The survey should be administered six months after use of Peer Coaching begins and thereafter at six-month intervals.

(If scantron or similar answer forms are provided, copies of the survey may be reused.)

For items 1–16, use this code for a scale on a scantron form:

> A = 0
> B = 1
> C = 2
> D = 3
> E = 4 or more

1. How many times was your teaching observed by your supervisor last year?
2. How many times were the observations used for evaluation?
3. Of the supervisor's evaluation observations, how many were followed by feedback conferences?

4. How many changes in your teaching occurred after evaluation observations?

5. How many times were the supervisor's observations "walk-through" observations?

6. How many "walk-through" observations were followed by feedback?

7. How many changes in your teaching occurred after "walk-through" observations?

8. How many times did an administrator other than your supervisor observe your teaching last year?

9. How many times did an administrator other than your supervisor give you feedback on your teaching after observing?

10. How many changes in your teaching occurred as a result of an administrator other than your supervisor observing your teaching?

11. How many times did you observe a fellow teacher teaching last year?

12. How many times did a fellow teacher observe you teaching last year?

13. How many times was the fellow teacher's observation followed by feedback or a conference?

14. How many changes in your teaching occurred after observation and feedback from a fellow teacher?

15. How many workshops, seminars, in-service training sessions, and/or staff development sessions did you attend last year?

16. How many changes occurred in your teaching as a result of attendance at workshops, seminars, in-service, and/or staff development sessions?

For items 17–25, use this scale:
   A = Poor
   B = Fair
   C = Average
   D = Very Good
   E = Excellent

17. I would rank the average overall rating of all workshops I attended last year as:
18. I would rate the quality of my supervisor's conferences after an evaluation observation as:
19. I would rate the quality of the changes that occurred in my teaching after an evaluation conference as:
20. I would rate the quality of feedback or conferences after a "walk-through" observation by my supervisor as:
21. I would rate the quality of the changes in my teaching that occurred after a "walk-through" observation and/or conference by my supervisor as:
22. I would rate the quality of observation and feedback from an administrator other than my supervisor as:
23. I would rate the quality of the changes that occurred in my teaching as a result of observation and feedback from an administrator other than my supervisor as:

24. I would rate the quality of a fellow teacher's feedback after observing my teaching as:
25. I would rate the quality of changes in my teaching that occurred after observation and feedback by a fellow teacher as:

APPENDIX 2

A TRAINING AGENDA
FOR PEER COACHING

TEACHING PEER COACHING IN STAFF DEVELOPMENT SEMINARS

LOGISTICS

Numbers for seminar: 24 or any smaller even number for pairing

Setting: a large comfortable room with adult-sized chairs and tables, plenty of light, and a pleasant atmosphere

Seating: 4, 6, or 8 persons per table

Ideal time: 8:30 A.M.–11:30 A.M. for each seminar

Refreshments: light and plentiful, open buffet table

Breaks: as participants need them, solo

Equipment: overhead projector, presenter's table, white or chalk board and markers

Materials: copies of Pre-Training survey and scantron forms, transparencies and handouts from masters in appendix 1, copies of the Joyce and Showers (1982) article on "The Coaching of Teaching" or Sandra Rogers's article "If I Can See Myself, I Can Change."

Books: a copy of *Peer Coaching for Educators* for each participant.

PRESENTERS

Ideally, two Peer Coaching trainers will present the sessions, taking turns. If only one presenter is available, another person (such as Roland Barth mentions) will act as that presenter's coach.

The two persons should be deliberate about setting up their own five steps of Peer Coaching for coaching the presentation. The group should see them conferring before the session begins on the Teacher Requests a Visit. It should be obvious during the seminar that one person is taking notes or data on the presenter's Request for coaching.

After the seminar is over, the presenter and coach can really impress the audience by conducting their (model) coaching session in front of the group.

Another fun part is to let the audience then participate in the Process Review with the two presenters, answering the fourteen questions and being constructively critical friends of the presenters.

BACKGROUND PREPARATION AND READING

About two weeks before the session, let each participant complete the Pre-Training Survey. One person must collect them before the assigned background reading is distributed.

About one week before the session, distribute copies of the Joyce and Showers article or the Rogers article for everyone to read.

SAMPLE PEER COACHING SEMINAR AGENDA

8:00 A.M. Refreshments available
         The presenters conduct their own Request for a Visit privately

8:30   Greetings, Introductions: presenters and participants

8:45   Discussion of Elements of Teaching chart
         Demonstration of a Skill without feedback and coaching: discussion

9:00   Definition of Peer Coaching and the Five Steps Mini-lecture on Theory

9:30   Demonstration of the Model: Peer Coaching: The two presenters model all five steps, using the scripted dialogue. The lesson should *not* be an ordinary classroom lesson nor should it last more than five minutes. (Adult learners have short attention spans!) Good sample lessons I have used include Taking a Fish Hook from Your Arm (using a potato, not a real arm), Chisanbop, Jump Starting a Battery, Fingerprinting, Hula Hand Gestures. The two presenters model the five steps in a lively fashion with no wasted time.

10:00   Guided Practice: Paired participants play role of coach and teacher. Having decided who will be coach first, pairs conduct the Teacher

Requests a Visit step. One presenter takes the role of teacher for everyone and teaches a fast, entertaining five-minute lesson, with the teachers of each pair acting as students. The coach of each pair gathers data, then reviews notes and lists some possibilitites. Coach and teacher pairs then conduct the Talk after the Visit, with the presenters critiquing the critical attribute, the first statement as the Talk begins. Each pair discusses the fourteen questions in the Process Review.

11:00   Guided Practice: The paired participants now switch roles and conduct Teacher Requests a Visit. One presenter conducts an even more entertaining lesson, taking the role of teacher for everyone. Again the quiescent teachers in each pair act as the presenter's students. Steps 3 and 4 should go much more quickly in this round, with the presenters circulating to critique more closely each pair's efforts. The Process Review can be done by the group as a whole.

Closure: Each participant enthusiastically departs with his or her first real Peer Coaching session scheduled. Just as in executive staff development seminars for administrators and business leaders, each participant receives a copy of *Peer Coaching for Educators* and a tee shirt with the logo: "Even Champions Need Coaching."

BIBLIOGRAPHY

Anderson, Robert H., and Robert J. Krajewski. (1980). Goldhammer's Clinical Supervision a Decade Later. *Educational Leadership.* February: 420–423.

Bacharach, Samuel B., and Sharon C. Conley. (1986). A Managerial Approach. *Phi Delta Kappan*, May.

Barth, Roland S. (1990). *Improving Schools from Within: Teachers, Parents, and Principals Can Make the Difference.* San Francisco: Jossey-Bass.

Berne, Eric. (1996). *Games People Play: The Psychology of Human Relationships.* New York: Ballantine Books.

Brandt, Ronald S., ed. (1987). Staff Development through Coaching. *Educational Leadership.* February: 3–91.

Caine, Renata N., and Geoffrey Caine. (1994). *Making Connections: Teaching and the Human Brain.* Menlo Park, Calif.: Addison-Wesley.

Cogan, Morris L. (1973). *Clinical Supervision.* Boston: Houghton Mifflin.

Covey, Stephen R. (1992). *Principle-Centered Leadership.* New York: Fireside.

Darling-Hammond, Linda, and Eileen Sclan. (1992). Policy and Supervision. *Supervision in Transition: 1992 Yearbook of the Association for Supervision and Curriculum Development.* Edited by Carl Glickman. Alexandria, Va.: Association for Supervision and Curriculum Development.

Fullan, Michael. (1993). *Change Forces: Probing the Depths of Educational Reform.* Bristol, Penn.: Falmer Press.

———.(1993). Innovation, Reform, and Restructuring Strategies. *Challenges and Achievements of American Education.* Alexandria, Va.: Association for Supervision and Curriculum Development.

———.(1993). Why Teachers Must Become Change Agents. *Educational Leadership.* March: 12–17.

Fullan, Michael, Gary Galluzzo, Patricia Morris, and Nancy Watson. (1998). *The Rise and Stall of Teacher Education Reform.* Washington, D.C.: American Association of Colleges for Teacher Education.

Garmston, Robert. (1988). A Call for Collegial Coaching. *The Developer.* August: 3–6.

Glasser, William. (1992). The Quality School Curriculum. *Phi Delta Kappan.* May: 690–694.

157

Goldhammer, Robert, Robert H. Anderson, and Robert J. Krajewski. (1980). *Clinical Supervision: Special Methods for Supervisors of Teachers.* New York: Holt, Rinehart and Winston.

Goodlad, John I. (1997). *In Praise of Education.* New York: Teachers College Press.

———.(1990). *Teachers for Our Nation's Schools.* San Francisco: Jossey-Bass.

Goodlad, John I., Roger Soder, and Kenneth A. Sirotnik, eds. (1990). *The Moral Dimensions of Teaching.* San Francisco: Jossey-Bass.

Gordon, Thomas. (1977). *Leadership Effectiveness Training.* New York: Putnam.

———.(1997). *L.E.T.: Leadership Effectiveness Training: The No-Lose Way to Release the Productive Potential of People.* New York: Putnam Publishing Group.

———. (1975). *P.E.T.: Parent Effectiveness Training: The Tested New Way to Raise Responsible Children.* Boston: New American Library.

———. (1987). *T.E.T.: Teacher Effectiveness Training.* New York: David McKay Company.

Gottesman, Barbara, with John Norton and Barnett Berry. (1993). *Changing South Carolina's Schools.* Rock Hill: Center for the Advancement of Teaching and School Leadership.

Gottesman, Barbara, with Phyllis Edmundson and Wilma F. Smith. (1996). The Language of Collaboration. *A Leadership Journal: Women in Leadership—Sharing the Vision* 1, no. 1. Summer.

Gough, Pauline B. (1987). The Key to Improving Schools: An Interview with William Glasser. *Phi Delta Kappan.* May: 656–662.

Hasenstab, Joseph, and Connie C. Wilson. (1989). *Training the Teacher As Champion.* Nevada City, Calif.: Performance Learning Systems.

Hord, Shirley. (1991). Managing the Change Process: Individuals, Innovations, Interventions. Presentation for the Center for School Leadership, May.

Hord, Shirley, William L. Rutherford, Leslie Huling-Austin, and Gene E. Hall. (1987). *Taking Charge of Change.* Alexandria, Va.: Association for Supervision and Curriculum Development.

Hunter, Madeline. (1993). Enhancement of Teaching through Coaching, Supervision, and Evaluation. *Evaluation Perspectives.* Western Michigan University, January.

———.(1988). Even Champions Need Coaching. Address at South Carolina PET Conference, Columbia, September.

Jensen, Eric. (1998). *Teaching with the Brain in Mind.* Alexandria, Va.: Association for Supervision and Curriculum Development.

Joyce, Bruce, and Beverly Showers. (1983). *Power in Staff Development through Research on Training.* Alexandria, Va.: Association for Curriculum and Staff Development.

———.(1982). The Coaching of Teaching. *Educational Leadership.* October: 4–9.

Levine, Sarah. (1989). *Promoting Adult Growth in Schools: The Promise of Staff Development.* Boston: Allyn and Bacon.

Lieberman, Myron. (1993). *Public Education: An Autopsy.* Cambridge, Mass.: Harvard University Press.

McCarthy, Bernice. (1996). *About Learning.* Barrington, Ill.: Excel.

Osguthorpe, Russell T., R. Carl Harris, Melanie Fox Harris, and Sharon Black, eds. (1995). *Partner Schools: Centers for Educational Renewal.* San Francisco: Jossey-Bass.

Palmer, Parker J. (1998). *The Courage to Teach: Exploring the Inner Landscape of a Teacher's Life.* San Francisco: Jossey-Bass.

Poole, Wendy L. (1994). Removing the "Super" from Supervision. *Journal of Curriculum and Supervision* 9, no. 3. Spring: 284–309.

Rogers, Sandra. (1987). If I Can See Myself, I Can Change. *Educational Leadership.* October: 64–67.

Sarason, Seymour B. (1993). *The Predictable Failure of Educational Reform: Can We Change Course before It's Too Late?* San Francisco: Jossey-Bass.

Schlechty, Phillip. (1991). *Schools for the Twenty-first Century.* San Francisco: Jossey-Bass.

Seldin, Peter. (1993). *Successful Use of Teaching Portfolios.* Boston: Anker.

Senge, Peter. (1990). *The Fifth Discipline.* New York: Doubleday.

Smith, Wilma F., and Gary D. Fenstermacher, eds. (1999). *Leadership for Educational Renewal: Developing a Cadre of Leaders.* San Francisco: Jossey-Bass.

Snyder, Karolyn J., (1981). Clinical Supervision in the 1980s. *Educational Leadership.* April: 521–524.

Snyder, Karolyn J., and Robert H. Anderson. (1986). *Managing Productive Schools: Toward an Ecology.* Orlando: Academic Press.

Sullivan, Cheryl Grande. (1980). *Clinical Supervision: A State of the Art Review.* Alexandria, Va.: Association for Supervision and Curriculum Development.

Torp, Linda, and Sara Sage. (1998). *Problems as Possibilities: Problem-Based Learning for K–12 Education.* Alexandria, Va.: Association for Supervision and Curriculum Development.

What Matters Most: A Competent Teacher for Every Child. (1997). *Phi Delta Kappan* 78, no. 3. November: 197–198.

What Matters Most: Teaching for America's Future. (1996). New York: National Commission on Teaching and America's Future.

ABOUT THE AUTHOR

Dr. Barbara Gottesman has been a teacher in grades 1, 2, and 4 and in pre-kindergarten. She has taught secondary and college English. She has been a K–9 principal and soccer coach. While she worked for the South Carolina Department of Education, she designed the NCSIE award-winning leadership development training, the Effective Schools Program, and the state effective schools surveys for parents, students, and teachers.

From 1990–95, she was the Executive Director of the state-funded, state-wide Center for the Advancement of Teaching and School Leadership, working with 150 school and university partnerships. She was principal author in the first version of *Peer Coaching for Educators* with Dr. James O. Jennings.

From 1991–98, she was also state site director for the South Carolina Collaborative to Renew Teacher Education, one of the charter members of Dr. John Goodlad's National Network for Educational Renewal.

Currently Dr. Gottesman is a principal in the consulting group, Education Connections–Synapse, and an associate professor in educational leadership at San Jose State University.

167503